TABLE OF CONTENTS

TABLE OF CONTENTS i

LIST OF ILLUSTRATIONS ii

CHAPTER

    1. INTRODUCTION AND BACKGROUND 1

    2. THE SIEGE OF PORT ARTHUR 18

    3. THE BATTLE OF MUKDEN 64

    4. CONCLUSION 107

ILLUSTRATIONS 123

BIBLIOGRAPHY 127

INITIAL DISTRIBUTION LIST 145

CARL CERTIFICATION FORM 146

LIST OF ILLUSTRATIONS

Figure	Page
1. Liaotung Peninsula	123
2. Battle of Nan Shan, 26 MAY 1904	124
3. Siege of Port Arthur (7 August 1904--2 January 1905)	125
4. The Battle of Mukden (23 February 1905--10 March 1905)	126

CHAPTER 1

INTRODUCTION AND BACKGROUND

It goes of course without saying that a frontal attack across a plain with masses can be made possible by greatly superior artillery.[1]

Lieut-General von Caemmerer, *Militar Wochenblatt, No. 147*

On the night of 8 February 1904, ten Japanese destroyers attacked the Russian fleet anchored at Port Arthur, Manchuria and began the Russo-Japanese War. Japan, a country that prior to 1853 was based on a feudal society, had transformed its military into a force able to fight, and eventually defeat a nation with the world's largest standing army. The conflict lasted until 5 September 1905, when the Portsmouth Treaty ended the war. In nearly every battle, the Japanese military defeated Russia on the field of battle.

Over the past ninety-plus years, countless articles and books reference the failure of the belligerent nations of World War I to learn from the lessons of the 1904-1905 Russo-Japanese War. In fact, the curriculum of the United States Army's 2002-2003 Command and General Staff College includes three readings that discuss the failed lessons learned from this war.[2] Each of these readings allude to one central theme: the failure of the world to accept the lethality of modern weapons as they relate to tactics and military thinking at the turn of the century.

This thesis will examine what tactical lessons were available to the international observers of the Russo-Japanese War. Numerous observers recorded the events of the war, with one author characterizing the war as a "dress rehearsal" for the Great War.[3] Another author described the war as a "laboratory for military experiments."[4] After the conflict, military and civilian observers published exhaustive reports on the war in journal articles, books, and after action accounts. This thesis uses these accounts to illustrate that the belligerent nations who fought the First World War did have enough information to forewarn them of the bloody battles to come.

To conduct this review, I intend to look at two major battles fought during the war: the Siege of Port Arthur and The Battle for Mukden. These two battles were selected due to their representative nature of the war and the size of the forces and material committed. These battles exemplified both spectrums of this war, with the Port Arthur attack representing a modern siege and the Battle of Mukden representing a large formation maneuver battle.

The Japanese attack on Port Arthur was the first large-scale siege in the 20th Century. This five-month siege demonstrated the lethality of weapons that later became prevalent in the battles of World War I. During these costly attacks, the combined effects of the hand grenade, trench mortar, heavy and light artillery, and the machinegun, were showcased. These same weapons would prove deadly on the battlefields of the First World War.

The Battle of Mukden was the last major land battle of the war and exemplified maneuver operations at the corps and army level. In this battle, Japan and Russia maneuvered armies exceeding 600,000 soldiers and integrated almost every modern weapon then known. The Japanese success in this battle allowed the country to enter peace talks from a position of strength.

In writing this paper, I intend to focus on the reports produced by the military observers present during the war. Many of these observers were to play significant roles for their countries in World War I. Lieutenant General (Sir) Ian Hamilton observed the war for Great Britain. He would later command the Allied landings at Galipoli in 1915.[5] Among the seventeen observers from the United States were John J. Pershing, leader of the World War I American Expeditionary Force and Peyton C. March, U.S. Army Chief of Staff in 1918. Douglas MacArthur, who would serve as the Chief of Staff and later Commander of the 42d Infantry Division in 1918 France, visited both Port Arthur and Mukden in 1905 while serving as his father's aide de camp.[6] Germany's observers included Max Hoffmann who orchestrated the German victory over Russia at the Battle of Tannenberg in 1914.[7] In addition to looking at the military observer reports, books and professional journal articles written soon after the war will be used to do discover what lessons were available, but simply not accepted for use prior to World War I.

Historical Background

Japanese interests in Korea and China date back to 1592, when Japan, under the dictator Hideyoshi, attempted to invade China through Korea. Over the next six years, Japan fought Chinese forces in Korea and at sea. In 1598, after suffering a major naval defeat, Japan agreed to peace terms and withdrew from the Korean peninsula.[8]

From 1598 until the opening of Japan by America in 1853, the Japanese demonstrated little interest in matters outside their home islands and tried to remain a closed society.[9] In 1853, Commodore Perry, using both threats and gifts, opened Japan to American and world trade.[10] At this point in history, Japan had two options for its future. It could remain inactive like China and become a target of colony hungry foreign powers, or Japan could adopt the means of western societies and move forward into the industrial age. Japan chose the latter and in succeeding years overthrew her history of feudal divisions and moved forward to a western style of society.[11]

Following European lines, Japan began a program of colonization and sought commercial interests of her own.[12] In 1874, Japanese troops landed on Formosa, but were later withdrawn after China agreed to pay an indemnity to Japan. In 1875, a Korean fort fired on a Japanese ship surveying the coast. Japan responded by sending a military force to Korea to avenge this attack. To avoid military action, Korea agreed to sign a commercial treaty with Japan that opened her ports to Japanese trade.[13]

The opening of Korea to Japan concerned China, which considered itself to have suzerain power over Korea. Japan, recognizing China's claims to Korea, sent a team to Peking to negotiate a commercial agreement. China, not desiring a war with Japan, agreed to sign a treaty with Japan that declared Korea "an independent country equal to Japan."[14] After this treaty, Japan built up its commercial presence in Korea, including a military force to protect those interests. China also placed troops in Korea and small skirmishes soon erupted. In 1885, Japan and China signed the Tientsin Convention and withdraw their military forces from Korea. Under this agreement, both parties agreed to notify the other if military forces were to ever be reintroduced into Korea.[15]

In 1894, Korea experienced a civil war and requested Chinese military assistance. On 4 June 1894, China notified Japan of her intentions to send troops at the request of the Korean Government. Japan seized the opportunity to further its interests in Asia and, within ten days landed troops at Inchon, Korea using the auspices of protecting Japanese citizens in Seoul.[16] Japan was determined to take this opportunity to strengthen its influence in Korea and, on 1 August 1894, declared war on China.[17]

The Sino-Japanese War gave Japan the opportunity to test its newly modernized military and foreshadowed the events of the Russo-Japanese War. In the ensuing eight months, Japan won a series of land and sea victories.[18] In September 1894, Japan secured its sea lines of communication by sinking four of China's warships and inducing the remainder of China's Navy to stay in port.[19] With free sea-lanes, Japanese units landed in Korea and later on the Liaotung Peninsula in Manchuria. In Korea, Japanese forces defeated the Chinese at the Battle of Pyongyang and later at the mouth of the Yalu River. On 21 November 1894, the Japanese attacked Port Arthur and within 24 hours the harbor was captured. Subsequent Japanese victories and the threat of a landing against the Chinese capital brought China to the peace table.[20]

The Shimonoseki Treaty, signed on 17 April 1895, ended the war. The terms of the treaty included the ceding of Formosa, the Pescadores Islands, and the Liaotung Peninsula, including Port Arthur, to Japan. Korean independence was also recognized. In addition to losing land, China was forced to pay an indemnity equivalent to 25 million British Pounds.[21] Japan's success over China and the capture of Port Arthur quickly raised Russian concern over Japanese expansion in China.

The presence of Imperial Russia in the Far East dates to 1860, when Russia gained territorial concessions from China and acquired much of Northern Manchuria, including Vladivostok, its first eastern port.[22] Like many Western countries in the 1800s, Russia desired to establish colonies in the Far East for future expansionism and commercial interest. To further these interests, Czar Alexander III began the Trans-Siberian Railroad in 1891 to connect the east and west expanses of the Russian Empire.[23]

Japanese control of the Liaotung Peninsula, as part of the indemnity from the Sino-Japanese War, concerned Russia who saw its Far Eastern plans being derailed. Russia desired control of the Liaotung Peninsula for two reasons. First, Russia desired control of Port Arthur as an ice free port for her Far East Fleet. Vladivostok, while offering Russia its first Pacific port, was ice bound up to four months each year. Second, Russia desired a foothold on the Chinese mainland to exploit what she felt was the eventual collapse of China.[24] Prior to the signing of the Shimonoseki Treaty, Russia sent a warning to the Japanese not to take any Manchurian territory as part of the peace settlement.[25] These demands were made public when *The Times* of London quoted a Russian diplomat who suggested a joint British, French, and Russian effort to reduce Japan's territorial indemnity from the war.[26] As a result of these demands, Japan did reduce the size of its land demands, but maintained control of Port Arthur as one of the requirements of the settlement.[27]

Soon after the signing of the Treaty of Shimonoseki, Japan was confronted by the combined interests of Germany, France and Russia, and basically told to withdraw its forces from Manchuria and Port Arthur. Japan, presented with few options, agreed to return the area to China with the understanding that Korea would remain an independent state. Japan also received an additional indemnity from China equivalent to five million British Pounds. Soon after Japan's withdrawal, Russia's desires for suzerain influence over Manchuria and Korea became apparent.[28]

To gain a stronger foothold in Asia, Russia established the Russo-Chinese Bank and loaned money to China to pay its war indemnity to Japan. In 1896, Russia and China signed a mutual defense treaty. In 1898, much to the chagrin of Japan, Port Arthur and much of Manchuria was leased to Russia for 25 years. In addition to this lease, Russia was given permission to extend a spur of the Trans-Siberian Railroad to Port Arthur.[29] To protect its interests in the area, Russia stationed troops at railroad stations along the route, which eventually grew into garrison towns.[30]

The 1900 Boxer Rebellion gave Russia a reason to bring additional forces into China. Under the guise of protecting its railroad and its workers, Russia increased its garrison troop strength in Manchuria from 2,000 to 12,000 troops. By 1904, this protective force, renamed frontier guards, had increased to 25,000 troops and was supported by six batteries of artillery.[31]

Russian commercial interests in Korea began in 1897, with the establishment of the Russo-Korean Bank. During this same period, Russian businessmen began a logging industry along the Yalu River. To protect these commercial interests, Russia deployed troops into the area. In 1898, at Japan's request, Russia entered an agreement to delineate each other's role in Korea. This agreement assured Korean independence and stated that neither country would interfere in Korea's domestic affairs. The agreement also stated that no military or civilian advisors would be sent to Korea without mutual notification and that Russia would not interfere with Japanese commercial development of Korea.[32]

Japan viewed this agreement as only a short-term remedy as Russia continued to build its influence in Manchuria and Korea.[33] In January 1902, in order to increase its security for future action, Japan signed the Anglo-Japanese Alliance. In this agreement, Japan and Great Britain agreed to maintain the "independence and territorial integrity of China and Korea" as well as securing "equal opportunities" in those countries for "commerce and industry of all nations." The agreement recognized Great Britain's interests in China, while protecting Japan's interests in Korea. The agreement also stated that if a third power joined in a two-party war against one of the signatories, the other nation would join the war against that foe.[34] With the Anglo-Japanese Alliance securing Japan against another joint European intervention, Japan began to focus on preparations for its next war.[35]

In April 1902, tensions between Japan and Russia continued to rise after Russia and China signed a new treaty further increasing Russian control of Eastern Manchuria.[36] In July 1903, Japan began a series of three diplomatic efforts to reach an agreement on a division of influence in China and Korea. The gist of each effort was a recommendation by Japan to divide the Far East, giving Russia control of commercial interest in Manchuria while giving Japan control of Korean interests. Over a five-month period, Russia refused to agree to any terms suggested.[37] On 13 January 1904, Japan made a fourth attempt to bring the issue to a peaceful conclusion. Russia refused to even discuss this fourth query and on 6 February, Japan severed diplomatic ties with Russia stating in an official message that Japan "reserved the right to pursue an independent course of action . . . to safeguard her interests and rights."[38] Two days later, Japan launched an attack on the Russian Pacific Fleet at Port Arthur.

Comparison of Forces

Soon after opening doors to western influence, Japan's military adopted a plan to become the preeminent military power in the Far East. To accomplish this goal, Japan chose to emulate the best military organizations of the period.[39] Beginning in 1867, French instructors began teaching members of the Japanese Army on western methods of warfare. That same year, Japan's first military academy was established.[40] In 1885, this instruction was augmented by the arrival of the first German instructor (this instructor, who trained many of the generals that served in the Russo-Japanese War, was personally approved by the German Chief of Staff, General Moltke (Sr.)).[41]

Japan began the Russo-Japanese War with a well-trained, professional Army. In 1904, the Japanese Army numbered 257,000 infantry, 13,000 cavalry, 13,000 engineers, and a trained reserve of 400,000.[42] As discussed above, the Japanese used a European model for its training and doctrine, with French and German advisors used extensively in the years prior to the Sino-Japanese War. To prepare for the possible war with Russia, Japan completed numerous studies on Russian strengths and weaknesses, including a study of the capabilities of the Trans-Siberian Railroad to support a Far East war.[43]

Japan's focus on military development is demonstrated by the large apportionment of its budget to this purpose. In 1895, at the conclusion of the Sino-Japanese War, Japan was spending approximately 26 percent of its Gross National Product (GNP) of $196 million on its military. By 1904, this expenditure was 31 percent of an increased GNP of $466 million, a 56 percent increase in spending.[44] In addition to this spending, Japan placed the majority of the war indemnity paid by China toward reorganizing and increasing its army and navy.[45] By 1904, the Japanese Army had increased from six to thirteen divisions. The Japanese Navy increased in size with the addition of six new battleships and six new armored cruisers, all built in Great Britain.[46]

While Japan placed a huge emphasis on improving its armies to western standards, Russia and the rest of Europe paid little attention to Japan's actions. When war was first declared, the standard observer believed Japan would be "crushed" by Russia.[47] Russia's leadership shared this perception of Japan, believing its military to be vastly superior.[48]

In 1904, Russia had an active army of 1,100,000 soldiers and a trained reserve of 2,400,000.[49] What Russia lacked, however, was a sound national will to conduct the war. While her commercial interests were fully committed to developing markets in the east, her military remained focused on the threats to the west.[50] As a result, only a fraction of Russia's huge military capability was committed to the Far East.

At the beginning of the War, Russia had 98,000 maneuver troops and approximately 25,000 fortress troops stationed in Manchuria. In addition, there were between 24,000-30,000 soldiers assigned to security detachments along the railroad.[51] Russia's primary weakness was its ability to reinforce its army. The constraint of a single-track railroad for resupply of both material and personnel impacted Russia's ability to seize the initiative throughout the war.[52]

As a fighting force, the Russian Army was in various stages of preparedness. The Russo-Turkish War of 1877-78 was Russia's most recent major conflict. In 1879, after a marginal performance in that war, a Military Historical Commission was established to gather and publish lessons learned.[53] In 1881 this reform plan ended with the assassination of Czar Alexander II. His heir, Alexander III, did not share his father's views of reform and returned the government and the military to an autocratic society. It was not until the late 1880s and early 1890s that histories and reports on the Russo-Turkish War began to appear in number.[54]

One critical shortfall in the Russian Army was absence of any requirement for academic studies to reach higher ranks. Much of Russia's officer corps, including all of its general officers, was promoted by favor and not abilities.[55] By 1903, only 30 percent of the army's regimental commanders and 50 percent of its division commanders were graduates of any advanced military education.[56] At the time of the war, the Russian leadership had a very superficial military education and was no match for the Japanese leaders.[57] This lack of advanced training for its military leadership in current military equipment and doctrine would play significantly into the Russian defeat in 1904-1905.

At the beginning of the war, the Russian Army was fielding a new quick-fire artillery piece (Model 1900, 3-inch) that was far superior to Japanese artillery.[58] These new artillery pieces were designed to absorb the weapon's recoil, thereby not requiring the system to be re-aimed after each shot fired. This weapon gave Russia a decided advantage in both accuracy and range over the Japanese.[59] The significant disadvantage for Russia in this new equipment was in soldier training. Many of Russia's artillerymen were new draftees who did not begin training with the artillery prior to loading rail cars headed to the Far East.[60] Additionally, the training manual for this new weapon was not published until May 1904, four months into the war.[61] Japanese artillery was inferior to Russia's, firing a smaller round a much shorter distance (3-5,000 yards versus the 6,000 yards of the new Russian artillery).[62] Japanese artillery was also of an older type that did not absorb the weapons recoil and had to be reaimed after firing. Japan's advantage in the war would be its use of artillery in an indirect fire role, using observers to direct fires from hidden battery positions. Russia on the other hand, placed its artillery in open positions that were quickly suppressed by Japanese artillery fire.

At the beginning of the war, neither army had large numbers of machineguns. Russia entered the war with eight machineguns per division.[63] At the initiation of hostilities, Japan had just begun fielded machineguns to its divisions.[64] As the war progressed, both countries increased their inventories of these decisive weapons.

Russia and Japan had comparable 5-shot bolt action rifles and both nations believed in the continued use of the bayonet. Their employment of the rifle, however, was significantly different. Russia still trained its force to use un-aimed volley firing by platoon and company.[65] The Japanese Army trained on ranges and became skilled in using one round to engage one target as it appeared.[66] The difference in the use of the rifle and aimed fire would prove an important factor in the war.

Summary

Japan entered the Russo-Japanese War prepared to fight a total war to gain control of Korea. Russia began the war unprepared to fight in Asia and desired to fight a limited conflict by committing only the minimum forces considered necessary to win. This lack of commitment throughout the first year and a half of the war hindered Russia's ability to gain the initiative and eventually set the conditions for its defeat.

The next chapters look at two of the decisive battles of the Russo-Japanese War, the Siege of Port Arthur and The Battle of Mukden. Each chapter begins with an evaluation of the troops and leadership involved, as these changed significantly between the two battles. One common characteristic that is found in both of these battles, however, is the lethality of the weapons used. Both Russia and Japan used the hand grenade, trench mortar, machinegun, and artillery in ever increasing numbers. During these two battles, Japan and Russia consistently adapted their tactics in an attempt to bring maximum firepower at critical points on the battlefield.

Written in a narrative format, these chapters use international observer accounts and professional journal articles as primary references. These chapters address what happened in the battles and what the observers recorded, highlighting the use of the weapons that proved so destructive on the battlefields of World War I. In both battles, the devastating nature of modern weapons is clearly illustrated. And in both battles, tactical lessons for the next war were clearly available to the observer nations to give warning of what to expect in the next war.

---

[1] Comment by Lieutenant General von Caemmerer (German Army) cited in *The Battle of Mukden,* trans. Karl Donat (London: Hugh Rees, Ltd., 1906), 71.

[2] These reading are found in CGSC's critical reasoning and creative thinking block of instruction. See Joseph Arnold, "French Tactical Doctrine, 1870-1914," *Military Affairs* (April 1978): 61-67, reprinted in U.S. Army Command an General Staff College, *I085 Critical Reasoning and I503 Leader Assessment an Development Readings Book*, (Fort Leavenworth: USACGSC, August, 2002), CR3.5-1--CR3.5-10; T. Travers, "Technology, Tactics, and Morale: Jean de Bloch, the Boer War, and British Military Theory, 1900-1914," *Journal of Modern History* 51 (June 1979): 264-86, reprinted in *I085 Critical Reasoning and I503 Leader Assessment an Development Readings Book*, (Fort Leavenworth: USACGSC, August, 2002), CR3.7-1--CR3.7-14; Michael Howard, "Men Against Fire, Expectations of War in 1914," *International Security* (Summer 1984): 41-57, reprinted *I085 Critical Reasoning and I503 Leader Assessment an Development Readings Book*, (Fort Leavenworth: USACGSC, August, 2002), CR3.8-1--CR3.8-11. A fourth reading on this topic is found in a history block of instruction in the Evolution of Warfare block (C600). See General De Négrier, "Some Lessons from the Russo-Japanese War," *Journal of the Royal United Service Institution* 50 (July-December 1906): 910-919, reprinted in *Evolution of Modern Warfare, Term I Syllabus/Book of Readings* (Fort Leavenworth: USACGSC, July 2002), 477-485.

[3] John English and Bruce Gudmundsson, *On Infantry* (Westport: Praeger, 1994), 6.

[4] Geoffrey Perret, *Old Soldiers Never Die* (Holbrook: Adams Media Corporation, 1996), 52.

[5] Ian Hamilton, *A Staff Officer's Scrap-Book.* 2 vols. (London: Edward Arnold, 1905).

[6] Edward Coffman, *The War to End all Wars, The American Military Experience in World War I* (University of Wisconsin Press, 1986), 12 and 162; Parret, 52.

[7] John Wheeler-Bennett, "Tannenberg," in *Decisive Battles of the 20th Century: Land-Sea-Air*, ed. Noble Frankland and Christopher Dowling (New York: Macay and Company, 1976), 24-35; reprinted *in I402, 20th Century Military History* (Fort Leavenworth: USACGSC, August 2002), MH2.2-1--MH2.2-9.

[8]William Maxwell, *From the Yalu to Port Arthur* (London: Hutchinson & Co., 1906), 1; Ernest Dupuy and Trevor Dupuy, *The Encyclopedia of Military History, from 3500 B.C. to Present* (New York: Harper & Row, 1977), 512-513.

[9]Robert Porter, *Japan, The Rise of a Modern Power* (Oxford: Clarendon Press, 1919), 55-78.

[10]Ibid., 79.

[11]*The Official German Account of the Russo-Japanese War, the Ya-Lu,* trans. Karl Donat (London: Hugh Rees, 1908), 1-3.

[12]G. Dickenson, *The International Anarchy, 1904-1914* (New York: The Century Co., 1926), 276.

[13]Porter, 116-118.

[14]Maxwell, 2.

[15]Stewart Lone, *Japan's First Modern War, Army and Society in the Conflict with China, 1894-94* (London: St. Martin's Press, 1994), 15-16.

[16]Ibid., 25-26.

[17]Porter, 132-133; Lone, 36.

[18]Edward Earle, ed., *Makers of Modern Strategy, Military Thought from Machiavelli to Hitler* (Princeton: Princeton University Press, 1973), 468.

[19]Porter., 134-135

[20]Approximately 240,000 Japanese were mobilized, with 174,000 troops actually employed on the battlefield. Lone, 52, 154-155 and 174-175; *The Official German Account of the Russo-Japanese War, the Ya-Lu*, 9-11. Porter, 136-139.

[21]Porter, 139.

[22]Julian Corbett, *Maritime Operations in the Russo-Japanese War, 1904-1905* (Annapolis: Naval Institute Press, 1994), 4.

[23]Sydney Cloman, "The Circum-Baikal Railroad," *Journal of the United States Infantry Association* 2 (October 1906), 53.

[24]R. Connaughton, *The War of the Rising Sun and the Tumbling Bear* (London: Routledge, 1988), 4-5.

[25]Porter, 140.

[26] Lone, 173-174.

[27] Ibid., 175.

[28] Corbett, 6.

[29] K. Asakawa, *The Russo-Japanese Conflict, Its Causes and Issues* (Boston, Houghton Mifflin Company, 1904), 83-88, 130-132.

[30] F. Sedgwick, *The Russo-Japanese War, A Sketch* (London: Swan Sonnenschein & Co., 1909), 4.

[31] Asakawa, 231-232.

[32] Connaughton, 9-10.

[33] W. Beasley, *Japanese Imperialism, 1894-1945* (Oxford: Clarendon Press, 1987), 76-77.

[34] Ibid., 77. Porter, 153-154.

[35] M. Kennedy, *The Military Side of Japanese Life* (London: Constable & Co., Ltd., 1924; Westport: Greenwood Press, 1973), 300-301.

[36] Porter, 154.

[37] Asakawa, 296-304., 335-336.

[38] Ibid., 337, 339-342.

[39] K. Riggs, Lectures: Russo-Japanese War, First Lecture, n.d., 2, Special Collections, Combined Arms Research Library, USACGSOC, Fort Leavenworth.

[40] Ernst Presseisen, *Before Aggression, Europeans Prepare the Japanese Army* (Tucson, University of Arizona, 1965), 9-11.

[41] Ibid., 101-106.

[42] Porter, 168.

[43] J. Ware, Discussion of the Influence of the Trans-Siberian Railroad on the Plans and Operations of the Russo-Japanese War of 1904-1905, Individual Report, 1931, Special Collections, Combined Arms Research Library, USACGSOC, Fort Leavenworth, 4-7; Arthur Ellis, "Compare the Russian and Japanese Services of Military Intelligence (G-2) to Include May 2, 1904," Group Report, 1930, Special Collections, Combined Arms Research Library, USACGSOC, Fort Leavenworth, 2; and Cannaughton, 12.

[44]Asakawa, 80.

[45]Rene Pinon, "The Struggle for The Pacific," *The Journal of the Royal United Service Institution* 325, trans. J. Clarke (March 1905), 295.

[46]Ibid.; Corbett, 6.

[47]Cyril Falls, *A Hundred Years of War, 1850-1950,* 3rd ed. (New York: Collier Books, 1967), 172; Porter, 157.

[48]Leopold Brooke, *An Eye-Witness in Manchuria* (London: Eveleigh Nash, 1905), 36; Ellis, 2.

[49]Porter, 169.

[50]H. Maguire, "Why did Russia Lose Her War with Japan?" Individual Report, 1930, Special Collections, Combined Arms Research Library, USACGSOC, Fort Leavenworth, 1.

[51]Bruce Menning, *Bayonets Before Bullets, The Imperial Russian Army, 1861-1914* (Bloomington: Indiana University Press, 1992), 153-54; Reginald Hargreaves states that the number of maneuver troops was less, placing the number at 83,000, and the number of troops assigned to security duty at approximately 30,000. Reginald Hargreaves, *Red Sun Rising: The Siege of Port Arthur* (Philadelphia: J. B. Lippincott Company, 1962), 20.

[52]Ware, 4.

[53]Menning, 88.

[54]Ibid., 95.

[55]Carl Reichmann, "Chances in War," *Journal of the United States Infantry Association* 1 (July 1906): 14-15; F. Kernan (Major), "Selection Versus Seniority," *Journal of the United States Infantry Association* 5 (March 1909): 700; and Sedgwick, 11.

[56]Menning, 102.

[57]R. Weber, "The Russo-Japanese War," *Review Militaire Suisse*, trans. Captain S. Bell, n.d., 212 and 219, Special Collections, Combined Arms Research Library, USACGSOC, Fort Leavenworth; and Reichmann, 14.

[58]*German Official Account of the Russo-Japanese War, The Yalu,* 58-59.

[59]Cannaughton, 20.

[60] Alexei *Kuropatkin, The Russian Army and the Japanese War,* vol. 1, trans. A. Lindsay and ed. E. Swinton (New York: E. P. Dutton, 1909), 274-282.

[61] Captain Niessell, *Tactical Lessons Derived from the Russo-Japanese War*, trans. G. Bartlett, n.d., 78-81, Special Collections, Combined Arms Research Library, Fort Leavenworth, Kansas.

[62] Denis and Peggy Warner, *The Tide at Sunrise* (New York: Charterhouse, 1974), 181.

[63] Kuropatkin, vol. 1, 307.

[64] Kurt Baldwin, The psychology, training, strength and armament of the Russian Soldier and Army, Individual Report, 1931, 4, Special Collections, Combined Arms Research Library, USACGSOC, Fort Leavenworth.

[65] Many of the draftees were 'Second Category' troops that had participated in annual training only, and were much older than the 'First Category' troops. Additionally, many of these second category troops had served prior to 1891 when the new Russian Model 91 rifle was introduced. Kuropatkin, vol. 1, 278-279; Riggs, Lectures: Russo-Japanese War, First Lecture, 11.

[66] Warner and Warner, 181-182.

CHAPTER 2

THE SIEGE OF PORT ARTHUR

No other nation will repeat the experiment, because men could never be relied on to advance under such conditions.[1]

Ellis Ashmead-Bartlett, *Port Arthur, the Siege and Capitulation*

This chapter looks at the isolation, attacks against, and final surrender of Port Arthur in the Russo-Japanese War. During this siege, the lethal nature of 20th Century weapons was clearly demonstrated. At Port Arthur, hand grenades, machineguns, crude trench mortars, and field artillery were consistently used to focus massed firepower at decisive points on the battlefield to gain success.

Recording the events of this battle were numerous international observers from almost every industrialized country of the time. Both military and civilian observers captured the events of the siege and wrote numerous books and articles about the fighting. In addition, several participants of the battle also wrote books and articles from first hand knowledge. Using these accounts as primary references, this chapter illustrates the lessons available to western nations prior to World War I. While it is not possible to review every aspect of the Port Arthur attack within the confines of this chapter, areas that illustrate the new lethality of combat, as discussed in observer and journal accounts, are addressed.

The Beginning of the War

Japan was fully prepared for the execution of the war and, within ten days of the surprise attack at Port Arthur, landed its first full divisions in Korea.[2] By 22 February 1904, eight Japanese divisions were ashore in Korea and moving north toward the Yalu

River. Using deliberate, planned maneuver, the Japanese Army quickly cleared Korea of Russian forces. On 1 May 1904, Japan attacked and defeated a Russian force of 6,000 troops in the Battle of the Yalu.[3] Within three months of declaring war, Japan had cleared Korea of Russian forces and set the conditions to conduct further operations into Manchuria and to seize Port Arthur.

The Japanese victory at the Battle of the Yalu in May was one of two preconditions for the landing of the Japanese 2nd Army on the Liaotung Peninsula in Manchuria.[4] The second precondition was the blockade of the Russian Pacific fleet at Port Arthur. This blockade was necessary to secure troop transports as they move Japanese forces to Manchuria. On three separate occasions, Japan attempted to block the harbor entrance by sinking outdated merchant ships in the port entry channel. The last attempt was conducted on the night of 2 May 1904, when eight ships were sunk in the entranceway.[5] This attempt proved temporarily successful, leaving Russia's Far East Fleet immobilized within Port Arthur for several days.[6]

On 5 May 1904, Japanese Marines secured a landing site in Yentai Bay (approximately sixty miles north of Port Arthur).[7] The following day, eighty Japanese transport ships began landing three Japanese divisions unopposed.[8] Within twenty-four hours, Japanese units moved over fifteen miles inland and conducted raids on the Trans-Siberian railroad and telegraph lines leading into Port Arthur.[9] By 13 May the Second Army, consisting of the 1st, 3rd, and 4th Infantry Divisions and the 1st Artillery Brigade, was ashore and ready for operations.[10]

Russia's failure to counter the Japanese landings in Manchuria exemplified Russia's weak military prowess throughout the war. Russia estimated that the Japanese landed a force of only 10,000 troops. Rather than strike the Japanese at its landing site where they were weakest, Russia chose instead to send guard forces south to protect the rail lines. A force of 4,000 troops, including four infantry battalions, a cavalry squadron, and a gun battery of four guns was sent to guard the rail lines ten miles from the landing site. Local skirmishes did take place, but no actions were taken to counter the landings.[11] While hoping for tactical surprise in the initial landings, the Japanese were astonished by the inactivity of Russia during the eight days it took to build combat power.[12]

Nan Shan, The Lethality of Modern War

The capture of the Nan Shan Hills on 26 May 1904 was a clear demonstration of the lethality of modern weapons when used in a prepared defense. During this battle, a single regiment in prepared defensive positions was able to hold the advance of three Japanese Divisions for twelve hours. In this one battle, Japan expended more ammunition than it used in the whole of the Sino-Japanese War ten years earlier.[13] The Russians were forced to retreat from Nan Shan only after the Japanese turned an exposed flank by literally wading through the sea to attack the Russian positions. Had the Russian leadership, which had adequate reserves available, committed a stronger force, the Siege of Port Arthur could have taken a different course.

The Nan Shan hills are located at a strategic isthmus thirty miles from Port Arthur and control the land approaches on the Liaotung Peninsula.[14] The hills rise to a height of 300 feet above sea level and overlook the northern approaches of the narrow isthmus and the small town Chin-Chou.[15] At low tide the isthmus measures 4,400 yards across. At high tide, the distance narrows to 3,500 yards.[16]

The defense of Nan Shan was the responsibility of Major General A. Fock, who was designed the Commander of the Fortified Zone. In this role, he was responsible for the defense of the Liaotung Peninsula back to the prepared defenses of Port Arthur.[17] To accomplish this mission, General Fock had over 20,000 men under his command.[18] Due to his poor military prowess and conflicting guidance, however, he committed only one regiment, the Fifth East Siberian Rifles, with 3,800 men to defend Nan Shan.[19] The remainder of his division was dispersed two to eight miles to the rear of Nan Shan.[20]

The overall commander of the Liaotung Peninsula was another weak officer, Lieutenant General A. Stoessel. Throughout the planning and development of the Nan Shan defenses, Stoessel gave Fock conflicting guidance on how to defend the site. This conflicting guidance was based on Stoessel's fear of a Japanese landing to the rear of the isthmus.[21] To counter this fear of a landing to the rear, General Fock ordered the commander of the Fifth Regiment, Colonel N. Tretyakov, to build positions behind his main lines, facing to the south, toward Port Arthur.[22] Even with the large number of troops available, Major General Fock made no plans to commit additional troops to support the defenses of the Nan Shan.[23]

General Fock further confused the defense by giving Colonel Tretyakov conflicting withdrawal guidance. After occupying Nan Shan, Colonel Tretyakov, one of the more competent Russian officers in the Far East, asked for additional forces for the defense. Fock replied to this request by saying that Tretyakov had all the forces he needed to *delay* the Japanese advance.[24] This guidance was later changed again, when on the morning of the Japanese attack, Fock told Tretyakov to hold the position "to the last man."[25] At the same time, Fock ordered his staff to locate fallback positions for the division when it pulled back.[26]

In 1900, during the Boxer Rebellion, the Nan Shan hills were fortified by Russia to protect Port Arthur against Chinese revolutionaries. After the rebellion, these sites were abandoned. When they were reoccupied in April 1904, the defenses were in complete disrepair. In the months following their reoccupation, Russia hired 5,000 Chinese workmen to assist in repairing and improve the defenses.[27] By the time of the battle, these positions incorporated many modern defensive techniques, integrating five tiers of trenches, land mines, over 5,000 meters of barbed wire, and two steam-powered searchlights for night surveillance. Additionally, fifteen battery positions were rebuilt to hold ninety field guns (varying in caliber from 56 to 150 millimeters). Ten machineguns were also integrated.[28] These defenses were considered "well-nigh impregnable" due to the fortifications and wire obstacles.[29]

The major deficiency of the Russian defensive plan was the placement of its artillery. At this point in the war, Russia followed the tactic of positioning artillery on the highest point available to provide observed direct fires to its maneuver units. No consideration was given to using the new long-range artillery in an indirect fire role or concealing their locations. Due to this faulty doctrine, Russian positions were quickly identified and destroyed by Japanese gun batteries, even when protected by earth dugouts.[30] Due to this faulty placement of its artillery at Nan Shan, Russia lost most of its guns by 9:00 A.M. on the first day of the attack.[31]

On 23 May, the Japanese 2nd Army, under the command of General Oku, began movement toward the isthmus at Nan Shan.[32] On 25 May, the Japanese were in assault positions, with 35,000 troops in three divisions supported by 216 guns, and forty-eight machineguns.[33] By 05:20 A.M. on 26 May, Chin-Chou was occupied and Japanese infantry began positioning for an attack on the Nan Shan Hills.[34]

At daybreak, Japanese artillery supported by four gunboats, opened fire on Russian defensive positions. Beginning at 8:30 A.M., the Japanese launched the first of several infantry assaults to capture Nan Shan. Japanese Infantry reached positions within 400-500 yards of the Russian defenses before being stopped by heavy small arms and machinegun fire.[35] In these initial assaults, Japanese infantry commanders quickly realized the effectiveness of machineguns firing from prepared positions. Throughout the day, Japanese commander's sent fire mission requests to supporting artillery to destroy machinegun emplacements that were stopping their advance.[36] Japanese artillery continuously fired on Russian positions, but was unable to destroy the machine-gunners in their entrenched positions. The Russian infantry, using only machineguns and rifle fire, were able to defeat each new attack.

During the battle, General Fock spent only a few minutes at the front and gave no support to the defenders. Even while Tretyakov's regiment was successfully holding the Japanese attacks, General Fock began sending a series of pessimistic reports to Stoessel, including a request to withdraw if the situation became "untenable."[37] At 4:00 P.M., General Fock dispatched two companies to Nan Shan to be used only "to cover a retreat" and not to be placed in "the trenches."[38] Early in the battle, after Colonel Tretyakov had lost most of his artillery, he had requested additional artillery support from General Fock. While Fock controlled another forty-four artillery pieces, he refused to provide any additional support to the Nan Shan defenders.[39]

By midday, after further attacks that included the commitment of General Oku's last reserves, the Japanese attack stalled.[40] At 5:30 P.M., as the sun began to set, a final Japanese attack was coordinated. To support the attack, General Oku ordered his artillery to expend their last rounds in an attempt to destroy the remaining Russian machineguns.[41] During this attack, the Japanese 4th Division flanked the Russian defensive line by wading through the sea and attacking the undefended sea approach to Nan Shan.[42]

Colonel Tretyakov, observing the Japanese flank attack, moved to that position in an attempt to gain control of the situation. At this critical moment Fock, who had continued to send lackadaisical reports to General Stoessel, received authorization to conduct a retreat from Nan Shan "if (the defenses) could not be maintained." General Fock took this as a green light to withdraw and immediately sent an orderly forward with a withdrawal order. The orderly could not find Colonel Tretyakov, so he delivered the message to one of the company commanders in the forward trenches. This commander, receiving an order from a general officer to withdraw, began to move his company to the rear. He also notified adjoining companies to do the same. Without any overall command oversight, the ensuing withdrawal turned into a rout.[43] When the Japanese observed the withdrawal, new attack was ordered and the heights of Nan Shan were occupied within an hour.[44] Colonel Tretyakov did not regain control of his regiment until after it had fallen back from Nan Shan.[45]

The Japanese troops were exhausted from the daylong battle and, with no remaining reserves, could not exploit their success and pursue.[46] It would be two days before Japan continued the attack toward Port Arthur.[47]

Japanese casualties at Nan Shan were approximately 4,300 killed and wounded.[48] The Russian Fifth Regiment lost approximately half of its force, with 1,500 soldiers and seventy-fire officers killed or wounded.[49] In addition to troop losses, Russia left behind sixty-eight artillery pieces and all ten machineguns.[50]

In hindsight, Nan Shan was extremely significant as a precursor to the later battles for Port Arthur. During this battle, a single Russian infantry regiment, with thirteen entrenched companies and ten machineguns, was able to hold off the attack of three Japanese divisions for over twelve hours. Had General Fock committed a larger force and additional artillery, this early battle may have stalled Japanese plans for some time.[51]

Japanese Attacks up to the Permanent Defenses

On 29 May, the Japanese advanced unopposed to the port city of Dalny. Located twelve miles southeast from Nan Shan, Dalny was built to become Russia's principal trade center in the Far East.[52] After the defeat at Nan Shan, the Russians hurriedly evacuated the city, leaving its docks, wharves, and a rail yard almost undamaged. Dalny would prove invaluable in supplying the Japanese during the siege of Port Arthur and also the Japanese armies in the north.[53]

After the occupation of Dalny, the Japanese Third Army was established to exercise control over the Liaotung Peninsula and to capture Port Arthur. Placed under the command of General Maresuke Nogi, the Third Army consisted of the 1st Infantry Division and the newly arrived 11th Infantry Division. General Nogi, who was present at the 1894 capture of Port Arthur, was called out of retirement to command the Army.[54]

The defining characteristic of the Liaotung Peninsula is the continuous pattern of hills and small mountains and the lack of any flat terrain. Generally, these hills run north to south, or perpendicular to the Japanese line of advance. Between these hills there are numerous narrow passes, ravines, and gorges. While the general lay of the hills offered the defender a limited advantage, the numerous passes and gorges through the mountains allowed the attacker the ability to cut off or bypass positions easily.[55]

The one of the tallest points on the peninsula was Chien-Shan hill, which rose to a height of 1,200 feet above sea level and offered the Russian's unlimited observation of Japanese movements. Russia's defensive line ran basically north south along the Chien-Shan hill range in what was called the "position of the passes."[56] General Nogi's first action after taking command was to order the capture of Chien-Shan hill and deny the Russians any further observation of his buildup of forces.[57]

On the night of 25 June, the 11th Division launched an attack toward the hill and, by 5:30 P.M. the next afternoon captured the hill.[58] To provide direct fire support in the attack, three batteries of mountain guns moved forward with the division. These guns were placed on a hill southeast of Chien-Shan and opened fire as the attack began. The defenders were caught off guard by the massed fires of the attacker and quickly retreated, leaving much of their equipment on the hilltop.[59]

The Japanese lost 158 men in the attack, a comparatively small number due to the natural strength of the position. The impact of bringing the mountain guns to lay direct fire on the hill apparently broke the resolve of the defenders.[60] Over the next week the Russians launched a series of piecemeal attacks to retake the lost positions. Each failed.[61]

From 5 July to 26 July, there was little change in the overall posture of the belligerent forces.[62] During this period, several new Japanese units arrived at Dalny and joined the Third Army. These included the Japanese 9th Infantry Division, the 1st and 4th reserve or "Kobi" brigades, another artillery brigade with seventy-two guns, and three batteries of naval artillery. Significant to these new forces was the arrival of the additional artillery including 4.7-inch naval guns, several 3.9-inch mortars, and thirty older, 4.7-inch bronze "siege" guns. In addition to Japanese artillery, twelve 3.42-inch Russian guns captured at Nan Shan were integrated into the Japanese artillery parks.[63] While the Japanese paused their attacks to integrate these new units, Russia devoted its efforts to strengthening its defenses, building over five miles of trenches. To man these defenses, General Fock committed eighteen infantry battalions, twenty-two scout detachments, fifty-four guns (placed in the hill defenses) and thirty-two machineguns.[64]

On 26 July, General Nogi began his next attack with a 180-gun artillery bombardment. For two days, three Japanese divisions and one of the Kobi brigade (approximately 60,000 troops) attacked the Russian defenses with limited success.[65] The combinations of machineguns, prepared trenches and the natural strength of the terrain defeated each Japanese attack.[66] At 1:00 A.M. on 28 July, the Japanese launched an attack that captured a critical hill along the southern defensive line.[67] A second hill was then surrounded and the Russian defenders withdrew.[68]

In a move that was characteristic of all successful Japanese attacks, these positions were immediately fortified with fresh troops and machineguns. These reinforced positions were able to defeat all Russian attempts to retake the hills.[69] The loss of these two hills, which were the southern anchor of the Russian defenses, threatened the remaining defensive line, and a withdrawal was ordered.[70] By 9:00 A.M. on 28 July, the Japanese were in possession of the entire defensive line. Japanese losses from the three days of attacks were 4,000 killed and wounded. The Russian losses totaled 1,400 killed and wounded.[71]

The Russian forces were withdrawn to their final positions outside of the permanent defenses of Port Arthur. These defenses extended along the Wolf Hills in the north and curved around to the hilltops of Ta-Ku-Shan and Hsiao-Ku-Shan on the southern coast. The Wolf Hills defenses were only partially completed, with trenches dug only at the base of the hills. No secondary positions were prepared that took advantage of the heights. Additionally, at the order of General Fock, the trenches were dug at the base of the hills, failing to take advantage of the heights and a tiered defense.[72]

On 29 July, General Nogi ordered new attacks to commence on July 30th, in order to deny Russia the opportunity to strengthen their uncompleted defenses.[73] Japanese artillery began movement at dusk on the 29 July and reached their firing positions at 2:00 A.M. Japanese infantry began moving to assault positions at 3:00 A.M.[74]

The new offensive took the Russians completely by surprise. The Russians offered little resistance and fled toward Port Arthur. By 12:00 P.M. the Japanese were in possession of the entire chain of the Wolf Hills at a cost of only 200 casualties.[75] Japanese losses in five days of attacks were between 2,500 and 4,000 troops.[76] The total Russian losses were 1,400, with over 600 of these occurring during their retreat from the Wolf Hills.[77]

The Japanese were now within a few miles of the permanent forts of Port Arthur. In a series of half-hearted and ill-lead defensive actions, Russia had given up numerous defendable positions and was forced back to its last defensive lines at Port Arthur. Many of the positions, especially Nan Shan, could have significantly slowed the Japanese timelines for their attacks.

The Defenses of Port Arthur

Planning for the Port Arthur defenses began immediately after Russia took possession of the Liaotung Peninsula in 1898. This plan was based on the assumption that a future war would be fought with either Great Britain or Japan and that the port would be cut off by sea. Construction began in 1899, with their completion scheduled for 1909.[78]

The sea defenses consisted of twenty-seven coastal battery positions in hardened sites. The batteries mounted guns ranging in caliber from 4.1-inch to 11-inch. Additionally, some of the battery positions were not only hardened, but had built in electric lifts to bring rounds to the guns from hardened magazines below ground.[79]

The land defenses were built into the hills that surrounded the harbor of Port Arthur. These hills are approximately two and a half miles from the Port Arthur harbor. Dividing the hills in the northeast is Lun-Ho Valley. Through this valley run both the railroad and main road that lead to northern Manchuria. The eastern hills begin at the Lun-Ho Valley and extend down to the southern coast. These hills are the most rugged of the chain and were the best defended. To the west of the Lun Ho Valley, the hill range is less rugged, but consists of steep hills that command the entire harbor. The most significant hill in this chain is 203 Meter Hill, which would prove decisive in the later destruction of the Russian Far East Fleet.[80]

The planned land defenses for Port Arthur were to consist of two defensive lines. The outer line was to have six permanent forts (each hardened with concrete and mounting four 150 millimeter guns), nine smaller fortifications (with bunkers and covered infantry positions), and six fortified artillery battery positions. The six permanent works and many of the semi-permanent forts were designed with moats or scarps (ditches) dug to their front. These ditches were specifically dug to force an attacker into the open as he attacked, as well as to counter mining attempts against the forts. The inner defense was to have four lesser fortifications (with bunkers and covered infantry positions) and a continuous line of trenches.[81] All defenses were sited to provide mutually supporting fires and make the seizure of any one position nearly impossible.[82]

When hostilities broke out in 1904, the land defenses were far from complete. Only three of the planned six permanent fortifications were finished. The remaining defenses were in various stages of completion.[83]

In March 1904, Lieutenant General Konstantin Smirnov, an extremely competent officer, arrived to take the position of Commandant of the Port Arthur defenses. General Stoessel remained as the overall commander of the peninsula defenses.[84] General Smirnov was shocked at the state of the defenses. General Stoessel, who had been in charge of the Port Arthur defenses for some time, had proclaimed as recently as January 1904 that the defenses were ready to withstand any attack.[85] Only the sea defenses proved capable of filling its mission of protecting the port from naval attack.[86]

To defend the fortress, General Smirnov had approximately 38,000 army soldiers, including 28,000 trained infantrymen. Additionally, 10,000 sailors from the ships in the harbor and another 5,000 administrative troops were added to the defender's strength. In all, the fortress had approximately 53,000 troops to man its defenses. Later, other noncombatants who lived in the port were added to this number.[87] Providing artillery support to the fortress was 646 field guns and howitzers and sixty-two machineguns. This number included the original 259 guns planned on the approaches and an additional 186 naval guns taken from ships in the harbor.[88] While most of the coastal defense artillery faced out to sea, some of the 10-inch and 11-inch guns could be turned to support the land defenses.[89]

Working for General Smirnov was Major General Kondratenko, who was designated the Commander of the (Port Arthur) Land Defense. After the arrival of Smirnov, these two officers immediately began working together to improve the harbor defenses. Using soldiers and contracted Chinese laborers, vast improvements in the defenses were completed by August.[90]

The defenses varied in quality and design. Barbed wire, relatively new on the battlefield, was in short supply.[91] To supplement this shortage, normal telegraph wire was used. While this wire was easy to breach, it proved extremely effective in slowing Japanese rushes.[92] To supplement the telegraph wire, heavy 1/4-inch wire was tied into the defenses. This heavy wire was difficult to cut and the Japanese had to order special wire cutters from Japan to breach it.[93] One of the more interesting innovations of the Russian defenders was the use of an electrified fence. On the eastern approaches, a line was strung in front of the other wire defenses and charged with a 3,000-volt current.[94] Russian infantrymen actually feared the wire more than the Japanese, who easily circumvented the obstacle by using wire cutters with insulated handles.[95]

Russia also used land mines with both command and pressure detonation fuses. Artillery fire often cut the lead wires of command detonated mines, so pressure detonated mines were generally preferred.[96] The actual destructiveness of these early mines proved more moral than actual, with few casualties being recorded due to their use.[97] To supplement mine and wire obstacles, Russia also used boards with three and four-inch spikes facing upward. These improvised obstacles were effective against the attackers when anchored to trench parapets.[98]

The placement of Russian artillery was to plague the defenders throughout the siege. In a manner similar to that at Nan Shan, almost every artillery piece not mounted in a permanent fort was placed on the summits of the defending hills. Apparently no thought was given to using artillery in an indirect fire role and, consequently, nearly all exposed Russian artillery was quickly identified and neutralized by Japanese artillery.[99]

Japanese artillery though inferior in range was entirely placed in concealed firing points.[100] On numerous occasions, Japanese artillery engaged Russian guns and either destroyed the emplacements or forced the gunners to seek cover and not return fire.[101] When firing at targets, Japanese batteries fired at objectives unseen by their crews in an indirect fire role.[102] This technique shifted the emphasis of gunnery skills from the senior gunner to the observer, who was responsible for adjusting the indirect fires of the gun lines on unseen targets.[103] To limit the damage of Russian counter fire artillery, Japanese battery positions were normally dispersed.[104] To ensure coordination was made between these dispersed batteries, the Japanese, beginning with the Battle of the Yalu, utilized telephones to coordinate fires.[105] When supporting an infantry attack, Japanese artillery fired on its assigned objective until the last possible minute before lifting fires, ensuring maximum suppression for the attacking infantry.[106] To place maximum firepower at the point of attack, the Japanese began moving artillery into its forward trenches. Mountain guns and other small caliber guns (seventy millimeter and below) were moved up into the head of siege trenches to support the infantry in a direct fire role.[107] In the November attacks, entire batteries of guns were moved into the trenches to support the infantry.[108]

The Russians were most successful in their use of machineguns. Integrated into almost every defensive work, machineguns were responsible for many of the early Russian defensive successes.[109] One observer of the siege placed the impact of the destructive fires of the machinegun as one of the causes of General Nogi's decision to turn to siege warfare.[110] Throughout the war, the Russian soldier would prefer machinegun fire to that of artillery.[111]

The Japanese began the war with machinegun detachments assigned to only its 1st and 2nd Divisions.[112] By the time the Japanese began their attacks in June, each division had twenty-four machineguns, and used these weapons to provide suppressive fire in support of infantry attacks.[113] The Japanese would continue to effectively use machineguns in the attack throughout the war.[114]

One weapon that reappeared on the battlefield during this war was the hand grenade. Historically, grenades had not been used in any great numbers since 1760.[115] By 1890, the British Army had totally removed grenades from its inventory.[116] The grenades used by Japan and Russia during the war were of an improvised nature, made by stuffing expended shell casings or metal cans with gun cotton and black power. They were ignited using a length of fuse and a slow burning match.[117] By the end of the campaign, the Japanese were using grenades extensively, often carrying their rifles in their left hand to allow easy access and use of grenades when needed.[118] Grenades were often the weapon of choice for the both the attacker and the defender during the siege.[119]

In addition to hand grenades, trench mortars were developed by both sides and used by the hundreds.[120] These weapons varied in diameter from five to seven inches and were made with bamboo or wood cylinders wrapped with rope for strength. The round was usually a tin can or an expended shell casing packed with explosives and propelled by a small bag of black powder. Ranges for these weapons varied from 250 to 450 yards.[121] The grenade and mortar provided the needed firepower for success in the close in fighting of trench warfare.

The First General Assault, 7 August--24 August 1904

Japan began its attacks on 7 August by attacking the Ta-Ku-Shan and Hsiao-Ku-Shan hills located to the east of the Russian perimeter defenses.[122] Russia defended these heights with four companies dug into a series of trenches near the top of each hill. These defenses integrated twelve field guns, defensive wire, a machinegun and mine obstacles. Both hills were natural defensive sites with steep approaches on all sides.[123]

The attacks began with an extensive artillery preparation by twelve artillery batteries.[124] Significant in these attacks was the first use of the "squared map" or grid method to control fires. This method was used throughout the remainder of the war.[125] The combined affects of massed Russian fires, defensive wire and mine obstacles, and a seasonal downpour defeated the first day's attack.[126] The following day the Japanese succeeded in taking the hills with heavy losses. During these attacks, Japan used hand grenades for the first time on a large scale to support its maneuver.[127] In two days of battle the Japanese lost 1,460 killed and wounded. Russia lost 450 wounded and killed.[128]

On 19 August, General Nogi launched attacks on both the eastern and the western defenses of Port Arthur. In the west, Japan captured 174 Meter Hill, the furthest northern point in the Russian defensive line.[129] On the eastern front, an attempt was made to take a small defensive work known as the Water Works Redoubt. The Japanese successfully captured the redoubt, but were quickly ejected by a Russian strong counterattack.[130]

As the attacks on 174 Meter Hill and the Water Works were underway, General Nogi finished his plans for a full frontal attack along the lines of the 1894 victory over the Chinese. In 1894, a one-day attack by 18,000 Japanese seized Port Arthur from 12,000 Chinese.[131] In 1904, the Japanese estimated the Russian defenders to number only 20,000 to 25,000, a third of the Japanese total strength.[132] Believing this underestimation to be correct and knowing that his superiors expected a quick victory to allow his Army to be committed to the north, General Nogi ordered an all out attack to begin on 21 August.[133]

Over the next three days, General Nogi launched a series of frontal attacks. From early dawn on the 21st until daybreak of the 24th, the Japanese literally hurled battalions and brigades against the fortress in an attempt to force a hole in the Russian lines to exploit.[134] The main effort of these attacks was unexplainably focused in the east, where the strongest of the Russian permanent fortifications were located.[135] In these attacks, two Japanese divisions succeeded in gaining possession of only two small defensive works at the base of the defensive line.[136] In the west, the remaining Japanese division seized a corner of 203 Meter Hill, the highest point in that section of the defensive lines, but were forced out of the position within hours by a strong counterattack.[137]

At the end of the day on 24 August, the attacks were halted. These full-scale attacks failed due to a number of reasons. By placing the main effort of the attack in the east the Japanese assaulted strait into the strongest Russian positions.[138] These defenses had the majority of the permanent works as well as numerous supporting trenches. Wire obstacles succeeded in slowing the attackers, while Russian machineguns and artillery were able to kill thousands of Japanese as they attacked.[139] In all, the attacks cost the Japanese an estimated 14,000-15,000 soldiers, bringing the total losses of the Third Army to 20,000, a third of its initial force.[140] Russia lost 3,000 killed and wounded.[141]

After the devastating losses from the failed frontal attacks, General Nogi adopted a siege framework to reduce Port Arthur.[142] Due to the strength of the Russian defenses, General Nogi determined his organic artillery and current siege guns were inadequate and requested heavy howitzers capable of destroying the permanent concrete fortifications within Port Arthur.[143] General Nogi also ordered his Army to begin digging the systematic trench works needed for the siege.[144]

The Second and Third Assaults, 19 September--30 October 1904

Over the next two months, the Japanese began a systematic siege plan. The first series of attacks by the Japanese would focus on capturing the Water Works Redoubt in the east and 203 Meter Hill in the west. The Water Works Redoubt defended a natural spring, a primary water source for Port Arthur.[145] The decision to attack 203 Meter Hill was based on its commanding position in the western range of hills. From 203 Meter Hill, most of the harbor is observable, including the docks and facilities.[146] The capture of this hill would later be the decisive point of the Japanese attacks. When the hill eventually fell in December, indirect fires destroyed the anchored Russian fleet in three days.

One advantage that the Japanese had over the Russians during the siege was the ability to replace losses. On 3 September, 20,000 replacements arrived at Dalny to reconstitute the losses of the August attacks.[147] Throughout the war, Japanese units were maintained at near 100 percent strength, while no replacements were available to the Russians within Port Arthur.[148]

The siege trenches dug by the Japanese were five to six feet wide and as much as ten feet deep. The width of the trenches allowed the Japanese to move men and equipment freely while the trench depth gave them protection from observation and direct fires.[149] To counter the Japanese in their trenching operations, the Russians could only fire artillery and direct dismounted attacks. Artillery had limited effect on the trenches, and Russia used the dismounted attack as a primary weapon against the Japanese efforts.

To counter the Russian dismounted attacks, the Japanese used machineguns and small bore cannon to cover the siege works. The Japanese also threw grenades at the attackers.[150] In an attempt to slow or halt the Japanese trenches, the Russians conduced nightly attacks against the Japanese, throwing volleys of grenades, firing their wood mortars, and even rolling large explosive charges down hills at the Japanese trenches.[151]

When the Japanese launched their second large-scale attacks on 19 September, the Japanese siege trenches had reached within eighty yards of the Waterworks Redoubt.[152] After conducting almost thirty-six hours of near continuous attacks, the Japanese succeeded in capturing the redoubt.[153]

This attack was an excellent example of the complexity of an attack against a prepared defense. The Russians held the position with three companies and two machineguns. While defenders did not have any large guns integrated into their defense, several small caliber thirty-seven millimeter guns were employed. Additionally, a new innovation was used. This consisted of a torpedo tube taken from a ship and mounted in the defenses. These tubes were used as a direct or indirect fire weapon, firing seventy-pound explosives approximately seventy yards. Fires from the surrounding heights also supported the defenders.[154]

In the days preceding the attack, Japanese engineers first cut the defensive wire protecting the fort, and then crept forward and cleared mines.[155] At the hour of the attack, while Japanese artillery laid continuous fires on the Russian positions as companies moved forward in platoon rushes. A furious barrage of machinegun and direct fire artillery met the attackers. The effects of this fire halted the first day's assaults. Artillery was then called in on the Russians in an attempt to further reduce the defenses.[156] That night, two attacks were launched. During the second attack, infantry, using large numbers of grenades, successfully entered the Russian trenches. After several hours of hand-to-hand fighting, the Russians withdrew and the site was secured.[157]

In the west, the capture of Namakoyama Hill, situated on the approaches to 203 Meter Hill, was necessary prior to an assault on 203 Meter Hill. After a ten-hour artillery preparation, two infantry battalions advanced against the hill. In the attack, the Japanese used large numbers of hand grenades to stun the Russians and seized a foothold on the summit. The Japanese immediately fortified their position with machineguns and were able to fight off several counterattacks. Following a second day's artillery bombardment, the Japanese were able to seize the remainder of the hill.[158]

The final objective in the western attack was 203 Meter Hill. While not built as a permanent fort, several months of construction had resulted in fully prepared defenses. These defenses consisted of two lines of trenches with integrated machineguns and wire. Defending the hill were 1,500 soldiers from the 5th East Siberian Rifle Regiment, the same unit that defended Nan Shan.[159]

On 20 September, the Japanese launched their attack on 203 Meter Hill. To reach the first Russian trench, Japanese infantry had to cross 600 yards of open ground. With the exception of one small element that actually entered the Russian trenches at the corner of the defenses, every assault was stopped by the combined power of artillery, machineguns and grenades.[160] After two days of assaults and 2,300 casualties, the attacks were stopped.[161] Russian losses in the defense of 203 Meter Hill and in the loss of Namakoyama Hill were 400 killed and wounded.[162]

During the month of September, the first 11-inch howitzers arrived at Dalny. These guns were removed from coast defense forts in Japan to support the Port Arthur attacks. A total of eighteen 11-inch howitzers would eventually be used in the assault. Upon their arrival at Dalny, these systems were moved by rail to the front and were then literally manhandled into their firing positions.[163] Each gun fired a 485-pound shell out to a range of approximately 9,000 yards. All guns were concealed when being placed. From their firing positions, they could range anywhere in the Port Arthur area.[164]

On 1 October, the first 11-inch guns began firing on Port Arthur and delivering desultory fire on Russian ships in the harbor.[165] These guns would significantly reduce the defenses of the Russians. Russian bunkers, initially built to provide protection against 6-inch artillery, were all susceptible to destruction from the 11-inch guns.[166]

On 26 October, the third general assault began.[167] This assault focused on seizing three permanent forts and three battery positions located on the northern portion of the eastern defenses. After several days of preparatory artillery fires, the Japanese launched assaults lasting three days. The Japanese were only able to capture one battery position and the advance trenches of two permanent forts of Erh-Lung-Shan and Sung-Shu-Shan. The Japanese losses in these attacks were 2,021 wounded or killed. While these attacks were failures, the capture of the lead trenches did accelerate the siege trench efforts.[168]

The Fourth Assault, 26 November 1904

After the failure of the third general assault to reduce any of the permanent forts, Japan redoubled its engineering efforts. The engineers not only continued to expand the siege trenches, but they also began mining operations against the permanent forts in the eastern defenses.[169] In the east, the Japanese continued their siege trenches.[170]

In November, the strength of General Nogi's Army was increased with the arrival of the 7th Infantry Division. To replace the substantial Japanese losses, additional replacements arrived at Dalny, including five new engineer companies. By 20 November, these forces were integrated, and the Third Army was prepared for a offensive.[171]

The objectives for the November attack were six sites along the eastern defenses (two permanent forts and four battery positions). Siege trenches had closed to within forty yards of one of the nearest forts and within 200 yards of the farthest.[172] One of these trenches was expanded to hold an entire regiment of Japanese infantry for the assault.[173]

To support the attacks, mines were dug on the edges of the scarps and charges fired to fill these obstacles with debris. This action allowed the attacker easier access to the outer walls of the forts.[174]

On 26 November, after a bombardment that included the 11-inch guns, the Japanese left their trenches to be met by a hail of small arms fire and a shower of grenades from the defenders.[175] While the Japanese did reach several initial trench lines, the Russians committed reinforcements at critical points and were able to retake their lost positions.[176] By the end of the day, the Russians using the combined affects of grenades, machineguns, wooden mortars, and artillery, were able to defeat the attacks of two Japanese divisions.[177]

That night, the Japanese attempted a clandestine attack to turn the flank of the Russian eastern defenses. Approximately 2,600 volunteers from the four divisions attempted to breach the seam between the east and west fortifications in the Lun-Ho Valley. At around 2:00 A.M., as this large force attempted to breach a wire obstacle, a Russian searchlight illuminated the force. In the ensuing barrage of artillery, rifle and machinegun fire, the Japanese lost an estimated 1,500 men of the attack force.[178] This failed attack ended the assaults in the east. The total losses for the Japanese in twenty-four hours of action were 5,500 killed and wounded.[179] After these significant losses, General Nogi turned his entire attention to capturing 203 Meter Hill.

The Capture of 203 Meter Hill, 28 November--5 December 1904

After the Japanese attacks in September, the defenders of 203 Meter Hill spent day and night rebuilding their defenses and turned the hill into a fortress. By the time the preparatory artillery attacks began, the defenders had made numerous improvements to the hill. Bunkers were constructed along the trench lines to protect the infantry from artillery fire, and a large bunker was built at the rear of the hill to hold a counterattack force. Two belts of wire covered the trench line approaches. At the beginning of the attack, the hill had five companies defending it with four machineguns.[180]

By the end of November, Japanese siege trenches had reached a point only forty meters from the forward Russian trench on the hill.[181] The 1st Division, the 1st Kobi Brigade, and the newly arrived 7th Division were assigned to conduct the attack.[182] After a significant artillery preparation, Japanese infantry fought their way up to the main trench line. They were soon forced back down the hill by Russian counterattacks, but were able to maintain control of the first Russian trench line.[183] Over the next eight days some of the bloodiest fighting of the war would take place to seize this one hill.

During the attack on 203 Meter Hill, the fires of the 11-inch guns proved critical for the Japanese. After several days of continuous fires, the 11-inch guns soon reduced every manmade feature on the hill into rubble, leaving almost no trace of the trenches.[184] Due to these continuous fires, the defenders resorted to manning the line with only a few scouts that would call for reinforcements from the rear of the hill at the beginning of a new attack.[185] The hilltop turned into a "no mans land," with grenades and machinegun fire raking every corner.[186] Over the course of the battle, Russia would lose an average of 500 casualties a day.[187] To replace these troops, companies were stripped away from the fortresses' other defenses, significantly weakening them.[188]

The turning point in the battle occurred when Japan realized that the Russians strength was its ability to reinforce the hill from the rear. To defeat this reinforcement route, six batteries of 36 guns were massed on the crest of an adjacent hill to place direct fire on the reinforcement route during the Japanese attacks.[189] The hill finally fell on 5 December when a Japanese attack of eight battalions was launched.[190] The total Japanese losses were between 10,000 and 12,000. The total Russian losses were 4,000 to 5,000 killed and wounded.[191]

The capture of 203 Meter Hill gave the Japanese the observation post it needed to direct fires on the Russian Far East Fleet within Port Arthur. Within three days, Japanese fires had sunk or immobilized all of Russia's remaining capital ships.[192] Following the fleet's destruction, fires were shifted to destroy Russian factories, warehouses and port facilities.[193]

Mining Operations to the Surrender, 6 December--1 January 1905

After the destruction of the Russian Pacific Fleet, siege warfare continued in the east. Japanese engineers continued to push toward the permanent forts with trenches and mines. After losing 203 Meter Hill, the Russians readjusted their lines, falling back to a series of old Chinese forts in the west.[194] The loss of personnel defending 203 Meter Hill greatly weakened the remainder of the fort.

In the east, manning of the defenses was reduced by almost half to build a general reserve for the fortress. This reserve force was pulled back off the defensive line, increasing the reaction time for a counterattack, should one be needed against a Japanese success. The poor placement of the general reserve hastened the fall of the fortress.[195]

On 18 December, the Japanese detonated two mines under one of the permanent forts and launched a new attack. The defenders fought for most of the day, but were finally forced from the position. The Russian reserve force was never committed, greatly contributing to the loss of the fort.[196]

On 28 December, two mines were fired under Erh-Lung-Shan Fort, another permanent fort, and the Japanese launched a new assault. The Russians fought tenaciously to defend the fort for eight hours before being pushed out of the position.[197] At this stage in the battle, Japan now integrated not only machineguns into its attacks but also light field artillery and mountain guns. The result gave the Japanese infantry maximum firepower at the point of the attack.[198] On 31 December a third fort, Sung-Su-Shan, was mined and captured in a one-day attack.[199]

On 31 January, Japan was able to use these captured forts as a jump off point to capture Wang-Tai, a central hill in Russia's eastern defensive line. The following day, Lieutenant General Stoessel sent a flag of truce to discuss surrender terms.

Summary

In looking at the accounts of the Siege of Port Arthur, the one prevalent feature in the observer accounts is the critical requirement to bring maximum firepower to bear during an attack for success. During the siege, the Japanese refined this tactic and committed all possible weapons in support of its infantry attacks. The free use of hand grenades and machineguns, as well as artillery and improvised mortars, proved necessary for a successful attack. While siege artillery and mining were critical to reduce the defenses, infantry still had to enter the positions to secure them.

Also clear in the observer accounts was the lethal affect of modern firepower on the battlefield. While losses of 20,000 soldiers a day did not occur in every daily attack as on the Somme Battlefield, losses as a percentage of the total force committed were extremely high. The Siege of Port Arthur cost the Japanese over 91,000 soldiers, roughly ten percent of its total army in Manchuria.[200] This number is even more substantial when compared to the total committed force of 75,000 to 90,000.[201] In this comparison, the Japanese experienced a one hundred percent casualty rate for its attacking force. The Russians, in the defense, lost 65,000 soldiers (killed and captured), including ground troops and naval personnel. Significant in this loss was the sinking of the Far East Fleet.[202]

The capture of Port Arthur was not the decisive act of the Russo-Japanese War, but was a strategic and moral victory for Japan. Strategically, the port was Russia's only ice-free harbor in the Far East. Located close to the Yellow Sea, it gave Russia the ability to interdict Japan's sea lines of communication as well as the ability to influence Chinese and Korean affairs.[203] Russia's continued possession of the port offered the threat of Russia joining its Baltic and Pacific Fleets to threaten Japan.[204] The moral value of the capture of Port Arthur was one of prestige and national honor.[205] By regaining the port, Japan not only justified the war, but also proclaimed to the world its superiority over Russia, but its preeminence in the Far East.[206]

---

[1]Ellis Ashmead-Bartlett, *Port Arthur, The Siege and Capitulation,* 2nd ed. (Edinburgh: William Blackwood and Sons, 1906), 471.

[2]Committee of Imperial Defense, *Official History of the Russo-Japanese War*, 2d ed., part 1 (London: Harrison and Sons), 1909, 45; J. Anderson, *The Russo-Japanese War on Land, 1904-1905 up to the Battle of Liao-Yang* (London: Hugh Rees, Ltd., 1909), 103; Maguire, 3.

[3]*The Official German Account of the Russo-Japanese War, the Ya-Lu*, 217.

[4] Oliver Wood, *From the Yalu to Port Arthur* (Kansas City: Franklin Hudson Publishing Co.), 29.

[5] A. Curtis, "The Siege of Port Arthur from a Naval Aspect," *The Journal of the Royal United Service Institution* 335 (January 1906): 58.

[6] At this time the Russian Far East Fleet's major elements consisted of five battleships and 6 heavy cruisers. For several days, large ships were sealed within the harbor. Port Arthur had substantial assets to clear the harbor entrance and with a few days had cleared the entranceway. Ibid., 60.

[7] Major H. Rowan-Robinson, *The Campaign of Liao-yang* (London: Constable and Company, Ltd., 1914), 62.

[8] Adolf Horsetzky, *An Epitome of the Russo-Japanese War of 1904-1905,* trans. Harry Bell (Vienna: Seidel and Son, 1915; Fort Leavenworth: Army Services School, 1916), 29; and Wood, 30.

[9] While rail traffic was interdicted by these raids, a final train containing weapons and ammunition (including 16 machineguns) did arrived at Chin-Chou on 10 May (en route to Port Arthur). On May 14th, the railroad was permanently severed when two Japanese infantry battalions and two cavalry squadrons occupied the railroad town of Pu-Lan-Tein northwest of the landing sites. Horsetzky, 30; Committee of Imperial Defense, *Official History of the Russo-Japanese War,* part 3 (London: Harrison and Sons, 1909), 11-12; Rowan-Robinson, 62-62; Wood, 30-31.

[10] These divisions were followed by the lead elements of the 5th and 10th Divisions on May 20th. *The Russo-Japanese War, Reports from the British Officers Attached to the Japanese Forces in the Field.* vol. 1 (London: Eyre and Spottiswoode, 1908), 81; Horsetzky, 32.

[11] Rowan-Robinson, 62-63.

[12] In 1894, Japan landed an invasion force only 30 miles from the location selected for the 1904 landing. While the Russian considered this location as a likely site, they placed no forces in the area to counter such an attempt. During the landings, no attempts were made by the Russian Navy to interdict the landings. Corbett, 220; Wood, 31; Rowan-Robinson, 63-64; John Ruckman (Colonel), *The Command and Administration of the Fortress of Port Arthur During the Russo-Japanese War.* Reprinted from *Journal of the United States Artillery* (November-December 1915), (Reprint undated), 27.

[13] Merion Harries and Susie Harries, *Soldier of the Sun, The Rise and Fall of the Imperial Japanese Army* (New York: Random House, 1991), 85. Total ammunition expenditures for the Japanese can be found in *The Russo-Japanese War, Reports from the British Officers Attached to the Japanese Forces in the Field.* vol. 1, 76.

[14]*Lectures on the Russo-Japanese War, Officers of the Japanese General Staff,* Translated by the American Embassy, Tokyo, 1906, 62, Special Collections, Combined Arms Research Library, Fort Leavenworth, Kansas.

[15]Anderson, 55.

[16]The difference landmass was made up of mud and sand that extended into the sea as much as 2,000 yards on both coasts and was considered non-trafficable on foot. *The Russo-Japanese War, Reports from the British Officers Attached to the Japanese Forces in the Field.* vol. 1, 65; Porter, 178.

[17]Freihen Tettau, trans., *Port Arthur, The Authorized German Translation from the Russian General Staff Account,* vol. 5, part 1, translator (to English) Walter Buttgenbach (Berlin: Unknown, 1910; Fort Leavenworth: Special Collections, 1912), 315.

[18]Major General Fock was also the commander of the Fourth East Siberian Division with another 16,000 –17,000 troops available. Ibid.; Charles Ross (Colonel), *An Outline of the Russo-Japanese War 1904, 1905* (London: Macmillan and Co., Ltd.), 162-164.

[19]This regiment, the Fifth East Siberian Rifles, was originally had eleven companies. Two additional companies were assigned day before the Japanese attack. N. Tretyakov, *My Experiences at Nan Shan and Port Arthur with the Fifth East Siberian Rifles,* (London: Hugh Rees, Ltd., 1911), 49; Major H. Knox, "Reserves in the Russo-Japanese War," *The Journal of the United Services Institution of India* 193 (October 1913), 404-405; and Anderson, 55.

[20]Rowan-Robinson, 71; Ross, 162-163.

[21]Ruckman, 27-29.

[22]N. Tretyakov, 15-16.

[23]Days before the battle commenced, General Stoessel changed his guidance again and told General Fock not to worry about a landing to the rear and to reinforce the Nan Shan position as one regiment "is not enough." General Fock only assigned two additional companies (for a total of 13) to support the Fifth Regiment in its defenses. Ruckman, 29; Tretyakov, 16; and Horsetzky, 30-31.

[24]Tretyakov recommended to General Fock to place two additional regiments on Nan Shan if it were to be properly defended. At this suggestion he was informed that he was only power hungry and wanted to command the whole division himself. Tretyakov, 8-9, 18.

[25]Tettau, part 1, 227.

[26] Ibid.

[27] Tretyakov, 7-8, 12.

[28] The exact number of field guns employed varies by account from 68 to over 100. Most sources reference 10 machineguns. Tettau, part 1, 202-207; Tretyakov, 21; K. Riggs, Lectures: Russo-Japanese War, Second Lecture, n.d., 16, Special Collections, Combined Arms Research Library, USACGSOC, Fort Leavenworth; and Footslogger (synonym, unknown) *A Short Account of the Russo-Japanese War, for Examination Purposes* (London: Forster Groom & Co., Ltd., 1925), 25.

[29] Ross, 158-159.

[30] Major E. Pottinger, "The Russo Japanese War," *The Journal of the United Service Institution of India* 158 (January 1905), 75-76; Major Niessell, "Cooperation of Infantry and Artillery in Combat," *Journal of the United States Infantry* 5, trans. William Snow (March 1909), 726.

[31] B. Vincent (Captain), "Artillery in the Manchurian Campaign," *The Journal of the Royal United Service Institution* 359 (January 1908), 33; and Ross, 157.

[32] While the three divisions of the 2nd Army moved south, newly arriving elements of the Japanese Fifth Division were ordered to move to Pu-Lan-Tien, 25 miles to the north to protect the rear of the Japanese forces. *The Russo-Japanese War, Reports from the British Officers Attached to the Japanese Forces in the Field,* vol. 1, 64-65.

[33] Tettau, part 1, 207.

[34] Chien-Chou was an old walled city. Two companies were used in its defense. Both were evacuated as the Japanese attacked the city. Tretyakov, 38; Wood, 31-32.

[35] While several accounts give credit to Japanese counter fire for silencing Russian artillery, two accounts place the silence on lack of ammunition. At the beginning of the attack Russia had approximately 160 rounds per gun. Riggs, Lectures: Russo-Japanese War, Second Lecture, 18; and Rowan-Robinson, 72-73.

[36] Pottinger, 76.

[37] Tettau, part 1, 234-235; Rowan-Robinson, 73-74.

[38] Tretyakov, 43, 50-51.

[39] The remaining artillery belonged to the 4th Division Artillery Brigade. Tettau, part 1, 215.

[40] The Japanese reserve was committed at 11:30 A.M. Riggs, Lectures: Russo-Japanese War, Second Lecture, 18.

[41] Rowan-Robinson, 73; Ross, 163.

[42] After turning the flank, the Japanese Infantryman scaled the cliff to the Russian positions and forced the Russian's to withdraw. Footslogger, 25; Major R. Burton, "2nd Essay Bombay Command, 1904," *The Journal of the United Service Institute of India* 163 (April 1906), 131; Pottinger, 76; and Anderson, 57-58.

[43] Tretyakov, 55-61; Rowan-Robinson, 73-74.

[44] Burton, 131.

[45] When the Fifth Regiment later entered the fortress, Lieutenant General Stoessel referred to the unit as a "wretched, undisciplined corps of traitors and cowards ..." for their loss of Nan Shan. This same Regiment and commander would be assigned the key defensive area on the western line (203 Meter Hill). Nojine, 84.

[46] Japan would commit its reserve time and again to win a tactical success during the war, and each time, would be unable to exploit that success with a pursuit. Rowan-Robinson, 77-78.

[47] *Lectures on the Russo-Japanese War, Officers of the Japanese General Staff*, 83.

[48] Pottinger, 76.

[49] Tretyakov, 54.

[50] Burton, 131; Riggs, Lectures: Russo-Japanese War, Second Lecture, 19; and Porter, 179.

[51] W. Eubank, "The Use of Field Fortifications," *The Journal of the United Service Institution of India* 163 (April 1906), 122-123; Ross, 163-164; Rowan-Robinson, 76-78; Tretyakov states in his account that will the additional support, the Nan Shan could have held the Japanese indefinitely. Tretyakov, 39.

[52] B. Norregaard. *The Great Siege, The Investment and Fall of Port Arthur* (London: Methuen & Co., 1906), 8.

[53] In the six years that Russia had owned the Liaotung Peninsula, 2,733,000 Pounds Sterling was invested into the development of the town. During this same period, only 491,000 Pounds were invested in the defenses of Port Arthur. Committee of Imperial Defense, *Official History (Naval and Military) of the Russo-Japanese War*, vol. 3 (London: Wyman and Sons, Ltd., 1920), 39; Wood, 39-41; Anderson, 94; and Footslooger, 25.

[54]General Nogi, as well as the Third Army Chief of Staff, were present at the 1894 capture of Port Arthur. *Reports of Military Observers Attached to the Armies in Manchuria During the Russo-Japanese War,* part 3 (Washington: Government Printing Office, 1906), 119; Harries and Harries, 85; and Horsetzky, 32.

[55]Norregaard, 14-15.

[56]*Official History of the Russo-Japanese War,* part 3, 14-15.

[57]Ashmead-Bartlett, 28.

[58]Tettau, part 1, 305-306; W. Smith, *The Siege and Fall of Port Arthur* (London: Eveleigh Nash, 1906), 87.

[59]Chien-Shan, was defended by four small caliber guns and two machineguns. Smith, 86-87; *Official History of the Russo-Japanese War,* part 3, 15.

[60]*Official History of the Russo-Japanese War,* part 3, 15.

[61]The Japanese quickly reinforced the positions after their capture. In three counterattacks, Russia lost 621 men. Major General Fock was responsible for organizing the failed counterattacks. Eleven companies from three regiments were used, but no overall commander was designated. A Japanese defender is quoted as saying the Russian attackers fell like "a row of ninepins" from the firepower of the Japanese defenders. Tettau, part 1, 312-313 and 320-337; Tadayoshi Sakurai, *Human Bullets, A Soldier's Story of Port Arthur* (Boston: Houghton, Mifflin and Company, 1907), 92.

[62]*Official History of the Russo-Japanese War,* part 3, 15; Smith, 93.

[63]The bronze siege guns dated from the Sino-Japanese War. Some of the naval artillery may have been 6-inch artillery. *The Russo-Japanese War, Reports from the British Officers Attached to the Japanese Forces in the Field,* vol. 2 (London: Eyre and Spottiswoode, 1908), 354; Norregaard, 20; and Smith, 93.

[64]Major General Fock placed primary emphasis to the north where the terrain was least restrictive. In the south, where the hills were more prominent little emphasis was placed on developing defenses. Rowan-Robinson, 161; Tettau, part 1, 343-44.

[65]The Japanese attacked in six columns with the 1st Division on the right (north), the 9th Division and one Kobi Brigade in the center, and the 11th Division on the left (south). The second available Kobi Brigade was held in reserve. *The Russo-Japanese War, Reports from the British Officers Attached to the Japanese Forces in the Field,* vol. 2, 365; Wood, 156-57; Tettau, part 1, 348; and Horsetsky, 96.

[66]Tettau, part 1, 355-356.

[67] Ashmead-Bartlett, 34-35; Wood, 157.

[68] *Official History of the Russo-Japanese War,* part 3, 22-23.

[69] Every gain made by the Japanese, including the capture of the heights of Chien-Shan was immediately reinforced with machineguns, new troops and often small-bore artillery. Tettau, part 1, 319-320, 366 and 373.

[70] *Official History of the Russo-Japanese War,* part 3, 23.

[71] Rowan-Robinson, 162. Tettau, part 1, 376.

[72] Major General Fock committed only one company to building the Wolf Hill defenses and ordered that trenches be prepared at the base of the hills only. General Fock had ordered a similar defense at Nan Shan (trenches only at the base of the hills), but Colonel Tretyakov, chose a tiered defense, which almost stopped the Japanese attacks. In addition to placing only ground level trenches, the Wolf Hills defenses were built at the edge of an un-harvested crop of Millet (or Kao-Ling), a Chinese grain that grows to heights exceeding five feet. Russian fields of fire were never cleared, allowing the Japanese to approach undetected up to the Russian defenses when they attacked. Tettau, part 1, 208, 344; and Tretyakov, 85-87

[73] Sakurai, 166-67; Wood, 157; Norregaard, 23; and Ashmead-Bartlett, 57.

[74] *The Russo-Japanese War, Reports from the British Officers Attached to the Japanese Forces in the Field,* vol. 2, 359.

[75] The Russians as they fled left large amounts of equipment, including rifles and packs. Russian artillery, in some cases, fired one round at the attackers and then limbered their field pieces and rushed to the rear, further adding to the confusion. Ibid; *Official History of the Russo-Japanese War,* part 3, 24; Tettau, part 1, 381; Asmead-Bartlett, 58; and Smith, 102.

[76] The British account gives the total at 2,500, while other accounts raise the totals to over 4,000. *The Russo-Japanese War, Reports from the British Officers Attached to the Japanese Forces in the Field,* vol. 2, 359; *Official History of the Russo-Japanese War,* part 3, 24; and Smith, 101.

[77] Tettau, part 1, 376, 385.

[78] *The Official History of the Russo-Japanese War (Naval and Military),* vol. 3, 35-38.

[79] For a complete review of the sea defenses see: *Reports of Military Observers attached to the Armies in Manchuria During the Russo-Japanese War,* part 3 (Washington: Government Printing Office, 1906), 171-176.

[80] Henry Reilly, "Port Arthur," *Journal of the United States Calvary Association* 63 (January 1907), 399-400; Captain L. Giannitrappani, "The Operations Round Port Arthur in 1904. Three Lectures by Captain L. Giannitrappani of the Italian Artillery," *Rivista di Artiglieria e Genio* (October 1906), trans. W. Carey in *The Journal of the United Service Institution of India* 167 (April 1907): 259-260.

[81] *The Official History of the Russo-Japanese War (Naval and Military)*, vol. 3, states that eight permanent forts were planned, while most other sources state that only six permanent forts were planned. *The Official History of the Russo-Japanese War (Naval and Military)*, vol. 3, 38; *Official History of the Russo-Japanese War*, part 3, 27; Horsetzky, 92; Barry, Richard, *Port Arthur, a Monster Heroism* (New York: Moffat, Yard & Company, 1905), 18; and Norregaard, 95.

[82] "Professional Notes, Operations of the Artillery and Engineers at the Siege of Port Arthur," *Journal of the United States Artillery* 2 (March-April 1905): 206.

[83] A 1905 article in the *Journal of the United States Artillery* states that the total planned permanent fortifications at six, not eight. H. Thuillier, "The Siege of Port Arthur," *The Journal of the United Services of India* 174 (January 1909): 57; "Professional Notes, Notes on the Defense of Port Arthur," *Journal of the United States Artillery* 2 (May-June 1905): 308.

[84] Throughout the remainder of the siege, Smirnov would have to answer to Stoessel, an officer who proved to be unsuited for the challenge of running the defenses. Major friction between the two officers became evident in August as the Japanese closed on the fortress. *Official History of the Russo-Japanese War,* part 3, 35; Freihen Tettau, trans., *Port Arthur, The Authorized German Translation from the Russian General Staff Account,* vol. 5, part 2. Translator (to English) Walter Buttgenbach (Berlin: Unknown, 1910; Fort Leavenworth: Special Collections, 1912), 11-12, 17-19.

[85] Nojine, 23-24.

[86] Throughout the first months of the War, the Japanese attempted several naval bombardments of Port Arthur. Each of these attacks was driven off by shore defenses. The Japanese were only successful in attacking ships at anchor with small vessels. Admiral Togo never allowed major elements of his fleet come within range of the Port Arthur coast artillery. Thuillier, 58; "Professional Notes, Operations of the Artillery and Engineers at the Siege of Port Arthur," 208; Andrew Moses, "Use of the 12-inch Mortar in the Land Defense of Coast Fortifications," *Journal of the United States Artillery* 3 (May-June 1907): 232.

[87] The total number of defenders varies by account, with few accounts taking into consideration the number of naval personnel at the port. The U.S. account in *Reports of Military Observers Attached to the Armies in Manchuria During the Russo-Japanese War,* part 3, agrees with the estimate of 50,000 combatants. *Reports of Military Observers Attached to the Armies in Manchuria During the Russo-Japanese War*, part 3,

123; Giannitrappani, "The Operations Round Port Arthur in 1904. Three Lectures by Captain L. Giannitrappani of the Italian Artillery," 267.

[88] The total number of artillery included land and sea batteries. Included in this number were 43 Chinese cannon dating to 1894. Thuillier in his account states that the number of naval guns dismounted was as many as 240, with guns ranging from small caliber 4.7-inch up to 8-inch. Tettau, part 2, 10; Thuillier, 58; and *Reports of Military Observers Attached to the Armies in Manchuria During the Russo-Japanese War,* part 3, 151.

[89] Thuillier, 58.

[90] Nojine, 25.

[91] Tretyakov, 126, 154.

[92] K. Riggs, Lectures: Russo-Japanese War, Seventh Lecture, n.d., 2, Special Collections, Combined Arms Research Library, USACGSOC, Fort Leavenworth; and Thuillier, 70.

[93] Smith, 257.

[94] Tettau, part 2, 5; *Official History of the Russo-Japanese War,* part 3, 31.

[95] Captain L. Giannitrappani, "Considerations on and Conclusions from the Siege of Port Arthur," *Rivista di Artiglieria e Genio* (October 1906), trans. W. Carey in *The Journal of the United Service Institution of India* 169 (October 1907): 526.

[96] Ibid., 527. "Professional Notes, Notes on the Defense of Port Arthur," 307.

[97] C. Collins, "Lesson to be Learnt from the Siege of Port Arthur as Regards to R.E. Work," *The Journal of the United Service Institution of India* 179 (April 1910), 303.

[98] Ibid., 305; The Japanese at times wore straw sandals versus their issue boots into the attack. *Official History of the Russo-Japanese War,* part 3, 31.

[99] T. Archdale, "Three Weeks in Manchuria," *The Journal of the United Service Institution of India* 168 (July 1907), 293; Harry Hawthorne, "Heavy Caliber Cannon In the Field," *Journal of United States Artillery* 1 (March-April 1908), 148-149; Tretyakov, 113; Smith, 100; Giannitrappani, "Considerations on and Conclusions from the Siege of Port Arthur," 528; *The Official History of the Russo-Japanese War (Naval and Military),* vol. 3, 61; Thuillier, 59; *The Russo-Japanese War, Reports from the British Officers Attached to the Japanese Forces in the Field,* vol. 2, 373; and Reilly, 419.

[100] To conceal their batteries, the Japanese would even move small bunches of trees to conceal positions if the terrain did not support hiding their artillery. Colonel Novikov, "Questions of Artillery Tactics from the Experiences of the Russo-Japanese

War," trans. by Fox Conner in *Journal of the United States Infantry Association* 4 (January 1908), 615; K. Riggs, Lectures: Russo-Japanese War, Third Lecture, n.d., 13, Special Collections, Combined Arms Research Library, USACGSOC, Fort Leavenworth; Niessell, "Cooperation of Infantry and Artillery in Combat," 726; Captain L. Giannitrappani, "The Operations Around Port Arthur in the Year 1904, The Development of the Investment and Siege of the Fortress," *Rivista di Artiglieria e Genio* (November 1906), trans. W. Carey in *The Journal of the United Service Institution of India* 168 (July 1907), 376; Giannitrappani, "Considerations on and Conclusions from the Siege of Port Arthur," 534.

[101] Major J. Cadell, "Theories as to the Best Position for Quick-firing Shielded Field Artillery," *The Journal of the Royal United Service Institution* 346 (December 1906), 1479.

[102] Major Niessell, "Cooperation of Infantry and Artillery in Combat," 744; Sedgwick, *The Russo-Japanese War, A Sketch*, 191; *The Russo-Japanese War, Reports from the British Officers Attached to the Japanese Forces in the Field,* vol. 2, 373; Giannitrappani, "Considerations on and Conclusions from the Siege of Port Arthur," 533; and Collins, 301.

[103] Captain Niessell, *Tactical Lessons Derived from the Russo-Japanese War*, trans. G. Bartlett, n.d., 82, Special Collections, Combined Arms Research Library, Fort Leavenworth, Kansas.

[104] Ibid., 84; *The Russo-Japanese War, Reports from the British Officers Attached to the Japanese Forces in the Field,* vol. 2, 373.

[105] Pierre Janin, "Notes on the Tactics of the Russian and Japanese Armies during the Campaign of Manchuria," trans. Arthur Williams, n.d., 67, Special Collections, Combined Arms Research Library, Fort Leavenworth, Kansas; "Professional Notes, Notes on Field Artillery Material, 1905," *Journal of the United States Artillery* 2 (September-October 1905), 168; Giannitrappani, "Considerations on and Conclusions from the Siege of Port Arthur," 534.

[106] Major Niessell, "Cooperation of Infantry and Artillery in Combat," 744; "Professional Notes, Operations of the Artillery and Engineers at the Siege of Port Arthur," 208.

[107]Horsetzky, 99; Tettau, part 1, 258; *The Russo-Japanese War, Reports from the British Officers Attached to the Japanese Forces in the Field,* vol. 2, 366, 384, 407; H. Hossfeld, trans. "The Russo-Japanese War," from supplements to the *Marine Rundschau* (1904-1906), 1906, 250, Special Collections, Combined Arms Research Library, Fort Leavenworth, Kansas; and Collins, 301.

[108]Tettau, part 1, 377.

[109]Giannitrappani, "Considerations on and Conclusions from the Siege of Port Arthur," 526-527.

[110]Smith, 185-190.

[111]Another author felt that the machinegun could even replace artillery in the defense "Military Notes," *The Journal of the Royal United Service Institution* 333 (November 1905), 1333; and Collins, 298.

[112]Niessell, *Tactical Lessons Derived from the Russo-Japanese War*, 101; *Reports of Military Observers Attached to the Armies in Manchuria During the Russo-Japanese War,* part 3, 106-107.

[113]Tettau, part 2, 343, 348-349.

[114]*The Russo-Japanese War, Reports from the British Officers Attached to the Japanese Forces in the Field,* vol. 2, 434.

[115]The articles "Hand and Rifle Grenades" and "Hand Grenades in the Russo-Japanese War," discuss the use of grenades during Napoleon's rule, and again in the 1866, 1864, and the 1870 Franco-German Wars. Use of grenades by the French and Russians at Sevastopol and by the British in the Sudan in 1884-1885 is also discussed. "Hand and Rifle Grenades," trans. from *Streffleures Oesterreichische Militarische Zeitschrift* (February 1911) in *The Journal of the Royal United Service Institution* 401 (July 1911), 915; and A Bortnowski, "Hand Grenades in the Russo-Japanese War." *The Journal of the Royal United Service Institution* 389 (July 1910), 918.

[116]Collins, 303.

[117]Niessell, *Tactical Lessons Derived from the Russo-Japanese War*, 111; *Official History of the Russo-Japanese War,* part 3, 168-169.

[118]The Japanese carried a slow burning match to ignite the grenades. The grenades would be carried on a rope around the shoulder with four or five attached or in a pouch.

Later in the war, an improvised percussion igniter was devised using a cartridge and a steel wire. Bortnowski, 919, 921; Ashmead-Bartlett, 139; and Smith, 255-260.

[119] At one point in the battle, Russia was making 2,500 improvised grenades in a 24-hour period. Russians often used expended shell cases from 37 millimeter guns for their grenades. Japan utilized everything from steel canisters to lengths of bamboo filled with explosives to build their grenades. Bartowski, 919; "Military Notes," 333, 1333; Collins, 303; *Reports of Military Observers Attached to the Armies in Manchuria During the Russo-Japanese War,* part 3, 192; Smith, 255-256; "Professional Notes, Notes on the Defense of Port Arthur," 308.

[120] Smith, 217; *Reports of Military Observers Attached to the Armies in Manchuria During the Russo-Japanese War,* part 3, 193; M. Kinai, *The Russo-Japanese War (Official Reports),* vol. 1 (London: Kegan Paul, Trench, Taubner & Co., Ltd., n.d.), 327.

[121] *Reports of Military Observers Attached to the Armies in Manchuria During the Russo-Japanese War,* part 3, 192-193; Smith, 214-215, 255; *Official History of the Russo-Japanese War,* part 3, 169-171; Bortnowski, 919.

[122] These hills were not part of the permanent fortifications, but were attacked in support of the first major land attacks. *The Russo-Japanese War, Reports from the British Officers Attached to the Japanese Forces in the Field,* vol. 2, 416.

[123] The Russians first occupied the sites on 3 July and had adequate time to prepare a more thorough defense. Tettau, part 2, 42-61.

[124] *The Russo-Japanese War, Reports from the British Officers Attached to the Japanese Forces in the Field,* vol. 2, 416-417.

[125] The Japanese had a squared map system for the entire Port Arthur area. To fire, batteries were called by telephone and give the square that needed to be fired. The grid method for controlling fires was used by the Japanese for the remainder of the war. The Russians later tried this same technique, but their attempts were unsuccessful. Giannitrappani, "Considerations on and Conclusions from the Siege of Port Arthur," 534; Captain Tiemann Horn, "Present Method and Lessons in Regard to Field Artillery Taught by the Russo-Japanese War," *Journal of the United States Artillery* 3 (November-December 1908), 257-258; Nojine, 148; Tettau, part 3, 22; and *The Official History of the Russo-Japanese War (Naval and Military),* vol. 3, 61-62.

[126] July and August was the rainy season in Southern Manchuria. *The Russo-Japanese War, Reports from the British Officers Attached to the Japanese Forces in the Field,* vol. 2, 350; and Sakurai, 175, 179-183.

[127] Tettau, part 2, 56.

[128] The Russian General Staff Account states the Japanese losses were 1,780. *The Russo-Japanese War, Reports from the British Officers Attached to the Japanese Forces in the Field,* vol. 2, 416-18; Tettau, part 2, 61.

[129] Interestingly, General Stoessel had personally ordered this hill fortified over any other in the defensive chain on 3 August. The more prominent hill in this chain was 203 Meter Hill, less than 1,000 yards to the rear. It was the loss of 203 Meter Hill in December that directly resulted in the destruction of the Russian Pacific fleet by indirect artillery fire. Tettau, part 2, 24; Both Smirnov and Kondratenko requested the additional defensive efforts placed on 203 Meter Hill. Stoessel overruled them. Nojine, 106.

[130] Thuillier, 59.

[131] Giannitrappani, states the number as 14,000. Giannitrappani, "The Operations Around Port Arthur in the Year 1904, The Development of the Investment and Siege of the Fortress," 372; and Lone, 154.

[132] The Japanese underestimation of the defender's strength continued to do so until the final surrender. As late as December, Japan believed Russia only had 600-800 soldiers left at Port Arthur. Norregaard, 47; *Reports from the British Officers Attached to the Japanese Forces in the Field,* vol. 2, 368, 405.

[133] Tettau, part 2, 16; Thuillier, 60; Earle, 470; Norregaard, 28; and J. Fuller, *A Military History of the Western World,* vol. 3 (New York: Funk & Wagnalls Company, Inc., 1956), 151.

[134] J. Kuhn, "From Port Arthur to Mukden with Nogi," *The Journal of the Royal United Service Institution,* 340 (June 1906), 799-800; *Official History of the Russo-Japanese War,* part 3, 46.

[135] E. Gunter, trans. "The Von Lobell Annual Reports on the Changes and Progress in Military Matters in 1904," *The Journal of the Royal United Service Institution* 337 (March 1906), 345.

[136] Wood, 163-164.

[137] Riggs, Lectures: Russo-Japanese War, Seventh Lecture, 11.

[138] Giannitrappani, "Considerations on and Conclusions from the Siege of Port Arthur," 531.

[139] The official Japanese account states that the attacks failed primarily to the effects of Russian Machineguns. Kinai, *The Russo-Japanese War (Official Reports),* vol. 1, 316; Giannitrappani, "Considerations on and Conclusions from the Siege of Port Arthur," 9; Giannitrappani, "The Operations Around Port Arthur in the Year 1904, The Development of the Investment and Siege of the Fortress," 377; and Smith, 188-189.

[140] Thuillier, 60; Giannitrappani, "The Operations Around Port Arthur in the Year 1904, The Development of the Investment and Siege of the Fortress," 377; Kuhn, 800; and *Official History of the Russo-Japanese War,* part 3, 50.

[141] Russian losses were estimated at 3,500. Riggs, Lectures: Russo-Japanese War, Seventh Lecture, 9; Rowan-Robinson, 168; In *The Russo-Japanese War, Reports from the British Officers Attached to the Japanese Forces in the Field,* vol. 2; and *The Russo-Japanese War, Reports from the British Officers Attached to the Japanese Forces in the Field,* vol. 2, 425.

[142] Thuillier, 60; Smith, 194.

[143] Horsetzky, 99.

[144] Smith states that the trenches would expand to over 100 miles. Giannitrappani, states only 32 kilometers of siege trenches were constructed. Smith, 238; Giannitrappani, "Considerations on and Conclusions from the Siege of Port Arthur," 531; Fuller, 159-160; and *Reports from the British Officers Attached to the Japanese Forces in the Field,* vol. 2, 363.

[145] The Water Works Redoubt was one of two water sources for Port Arthur. Japan mistakenly thought this was the only and primary source of drinking water. Tettau, part 2, 260-261; Giannitrappani, "Considerations on and Conclusions from the Siege of Port Arthur," 530.

[146] Reilly, 415.

[147] Giannitrappani and Smith both state the number to be 16,000. Giannitrappani, "The Operations Around Port Arthur in the Year 1904, The Development of the Investment and Siege of the Fortress," 378; Smith, 207; *Reports of Military Observers Attached to the Armies in Manchuria During the Russo-Japanese War,* part 3, 124; Hossfeld, 268.

[148] Even in the North with access to the Trans-Siberian Railroad for resupply, Russian forces were only maintained at roughly 70 percent strength. Gunter, E., trans. "The Von Lobell Annual Reports on the Changes and Progress in Military Matters in 1904," *The Journal of the Royal United Service Institution* 336 (February 1906): 228; and Giannitrappani, (Captain), "The Operations Round Port Arthur in 1904. Three Lectures by Captain L. Giannitrappani of the Italian Artillery," 268.

[149] Smith, 238; Horsetzky, 99.

[150] *Reports of Military Observers Attached to the Armies in Manchuria During the Russo-Japanese War,* part 3, 140.

[151] At the beginning of the siege, Lieutenant General Stoessel actually reprimanded a junior officer for conducting an attack on a siege trench for endangering the lives of his men. Only later was he convinced that these attacks were necessary to slow the Japanese efforts. Nojine, 192; Giannitrappani, "Considerations on and Conclusions from the Siege of Port Arthur,"526-527; Smith, 218; Nojine, 198, 230; Tettau, part 1, 389; Horsetzky, 99; and "Professional Notes, Notes on the Defense of Port Arthur," 308.

[152] Fuller, 160.

[153] *The Russo-Japanese War, Reports from the British Officers Attached to the Japanese Forces in the Field,* vol. 2, 429-431.

[154] Torpedo tubes were employed at eight other sites, including 203 Meter Hill. Committee of Imperial Defense, *Official History (Naval and Military) of the Russo-Japanese War,* vol. 2 (London: Wyman and Sons, Ltd., 1912), 527; and "Professional Notes, Operations of the Artillery and Engineers at the Siege of Port Arthur," 209.

[155] Ashmead-Bartlett, 152.

[156] Norregaard, 153.

[157] Ibid.

[158] *The Russo-Japanese War, Reports from the British Officers Attached to the Japanese Forces in the Field,* vol. 2, 435-436; Tretyakov, 171-175.

[159] *Official History of the Russo-Japanese War,* part 3, 61.

[160] The one Japanese element that did enter the Russian trenches brought two machineguns. Over the next two days, this element, of unknown size, defeated every attempt to dislodge it. It was finally destroyed after a group of Russian volunteers sneaked up on the Japanese on the night of 23 September and rolled a series of 15 pound bombs into the defender's trench. Ibid., 61-62; *The Russo-Japanese War, Reports from the British Officers Attached to the Japanese Forces in the Field,* vol. 2, 364.

[161] Smith states the number lost in the attacks on 203 Meter Hill was 2,000, with the capture of Namakoyama costing 200 casualties. Smith, 235; Thuillier, 61; *The Russo-Japanese War, Reports from the British Officers Attached to the Japanese Forces in the Field,* vol. 2, 364.

[162] Tretyakov, 181.

[163]Hawthorne, 148; Smith, 240-243.

[164]Norregaard, 173; "Professional Notes, Operations of the Artillery and Engineers at the Siege of Port Arthur," 206; *The Russo-Japanese War, Reports from the British Officers Attached to the Japanese Forces in the Field,* vol. 2, 383.

[165]A Russian battleship was hit with 11-inch fires on 2 October. Smith, 245; *The Russo-Japanese War, Reports from the British Officers Attached to the Japanese Forces in the Field,* vol. 2, 364.

[166]Riggs, Lectures: Russo-Japanese War, Seventh Lecture, 3; "Professional Notes, Operations of the Artillery and Engineers at the Siege of Port Arthur," 208; *Official History of the Russo-Japanese War,* part 3, 33.

[167]A limited attack was launched on October 16th, supported by fires of six 11-inch guns. After a one and one half-hour artillery bombardment, Japanese infantry were able to quickly capture a battery position in the east. Due the massive artillery fires and lightning attack, Japan lost only 150 soldiers in this attack. *Reports of Military Observers Attached to the Armies in Manchuria During the Russo-Japanese War,* part 3, 125.

[168]Riggs states that the Japanese lost 3,600 in attacks. Riggs, Lectures: Russo-Japanese War, Seventh Lecture, 13; *Reports of Military Observers Attached to the Armies in Manchuria During the Russo-Japanese War,* part 3, 128-129.

[169]Giannitrappani, "The Operations Around Port Arthur in the Year 1904, The Development of the Investment and Siege of the Fortress," 380-381.

[170]Thuillier, 64-65.

[171]Three companies arrived from the Japanese Armies operating in the north. Two more were reserve companies arriving from Japan. Thuillier, 65; Horsetzky, 102; and *The Russo-Japanese War, Reports from the British Officers Attached to the Japanese Forces in the Field,* vol. 2, 366.

[172]*Official History of the Russo-Japanese War,* part 3, 81.

[173]Smith, 329.

[174]*Reports of Military Observers Attached to the Armies in Manchuria During the Russo-Japanese War,* part 3, 131; Kinai, *The Russo-Japanese War (Official Reports),* vol. 1, 328.

[175]Thuillier, 65..

[176]Ibid., 337-345; Weber, 169.

[177] *Reports from the British Officers Attached to the Japanese Forces in the Field.* vol. 2, 367; *Official History (Naval and Military) of the Russo-Japanese War,* vol. 2, 589-594; Kinai, *The Russo-Japanese War (Official Reports),* vol. 1, 327; *Reports of Military Observers Attached to the Armies in Manchuria During the Russo-Japanese War,* part 3, 132.

[178] Nojine, 239; *Reports of Military Observers Attached to the Armies in Manchuria During the Russo-Japanese War,* part 3, 132-133; Kinai, *The Russo-Japanese War (Official Reports),* vol. 1, 337; *Reports from the British Officers Attached to the Japanese Forces in the Field.* vol. 2, 466; *Official History (Naval and Military) of the Russo-Japanese War,* vol. 2, 596-598.

[179] *Official History (Naval and Military) of the Russo-Japanese War,* vol. 2, 598.

[180] Tretyakov, 217-218.

[181] A "normal" siege trench proceeded at a speed of 2-4 feet every hour. Due to the rocky soil on 203 Meter Hill, these trenches moved at a much slower pace. Tretyakov, 207; and Horsetzky, 103.

[182] The 9th Division was committed within 24 hours of the first assaults. Norregaard, 252; Ashmead-Bartlett, 318; and Smith, 356.

[183] Smith, 354; *Reports from the British Officers Attached to the Japanese Forces in the Field,* vol. 2, 367; Thuillier, 65.

[184] Within the first days of the attack, 40 of 42 bunkers on 203 Meter Hill were damaged by fires. Over the following days, the entire hilltop was slowed reduced to ruble. Up to 4,000 rounds of 11-inch fire landed on 203 Meter Hill. The Russian account states the number at 1,500, while observers with the Japanese Army claimed the number to be 4,000 (Tettau, part 2, 426, 428; Horsetsky, 103; Norregaard, 248). During the entire war, these 11-inch guns would fire 15,000 rounds at the Russians (Fuller, 160). Reilly, 414; *Official History (Naval and Military) of the Russo-Japanese War,* vol. 2, 618; and *Official History of the Russo-Japanese War,* part 3, 94.

[185] Smith, 360-361; Ashmead-Bartlett, 319.

[186] Colonel Tretyakov, who commanded from the hilltop during most of the battle, and B. Norregaard and W. Smith, civilian observers with the Japanese give excellent accounts of the fighting to take the hill. Tretyakov, 230-256; Norregaard, 246-258; and Smith, 349-367.

[187] These casualties equaled 2-3 companies a day. Tretyakov, 243.

[188] Nojine, 250; Tretyakov, 282.

[189] Smith, 363-364; *Reports of Military Observers Attached to the Armies in Manchuria During the Russo-Japanese War,* part 3, 138; Thuillier, 66.

[190] Giannitrappani, "The Operations Around Port Arthur in the Year 1904, The Development of the Investment and Siege of the Fortress," 381.

[191] Total Russian losses vary by account. The British Officer reports report losses at 7,000 to 8,000. *The Russo-Japanese War, Reports from the British Officers Attached to the Japanese Forces in the Field,* vol. 2, 368; Other accounts record losses between 1,500 and 5,000. *Official History of the Russo-Japanese War,* part 3, 98; Nojine, 258; Tretyakov, 272; and Giannitrappani, "The Operations Around Port Arthur in the Year 1904, The Development of the Investment and Siege of the Fortress," 365.

[192] "Professional Notes, Operations of the Artillery and Engineers at the Siege of Port Arthur," 208; "Professional Notes, Damaged Russian Warships at Port Arthur," gives an overview of the damage sustained by the Russian Far East Fleet from the 11-inch fires. "Professional Notes, Damaged Russian Warships at Port Arthur," *Journal of the United States Artillery* 2 (September-October 1905), 174-178.

[193] Within the confines of Port Arthur the Russian's had established munitions factories that in addition to building thousands of grenades and numerous trench mortars, also built shells for artillery and refurbishing unexploded rounds fired by the Japanese. Several references discuss the reuse of ordnance including unexploded 11-inch rounds fired at the Russians. Smith, 305-306; Tretyakov, 204-205; Riggs, Lectures: Russo-Japanese War, Seventh Lecture, 15; *Official History of the Russo-Japanese War,* part 3, 82; and Curtis, 71.

[194] Tretyakov, 282.

[195] General Fock, took overall command of the Port Arthur defenses on 15 December after the previous commander, Major General Kondratenko was killed. Kontratenko was killed when an 11-inch round pierced a bunker in one of the permanent forts in the east. The loss of Kondratenko (who was known as the Hero of Port Arthur due to his efforts) and his replacement by Fock greatly increased the speed of the fall of Port Arthur. Lieutenant General Smirnov fought to keep Fock out of the position, but was overruled by Stoessel. Nojine, 276-284; Kuropatkin, vol. 1, 300; Tretyakov, 287; Porter, 201; and Norregaard, 292.

[196] Thuillier, 66-67.

[197] Ibid., 67.

[198] One company was sent for the Port Arthur reserve force to reinforce the defenders of this fort. This effort was not enough to save the fort from the Japanese attacks. Nojine, 286, 302; German General Staff, *Pamphlet 37-38, Individual Contributions to the History of Wars, Port Arthur,* Paul Brockmann, trans. Berlin: Ernst Siegfried Vittler & Son, 1906; Fort Leavenworth: Combined Arms Research Library, Special Collections, 1907, 118;

Reports of Military Observers Attached to the Armies in Manchuria During the Russo-Japanese War, part 3, 140, 183-184; *The Russo-Japanese War, Reports from the British Officers Attached to the Japanese Forces in the Field,* vol. 2, 366.

[199] Smith, 424-426; Greenwood, 74.

[200] These numbers include 57,780 killed, wounded and missing, and 33,769 soldiers designated as sick from various illnesses. A later account by Warner agrees with these numbers. *Official History of the Russo-Japanese War,* part 3, 133; Warner and Warner, 479.

[201] The definitive number soldiers committed vary in the observer accounts. The U.S. account, which is one of the most detailed, places the number at 75,000. War Department, Office of the Chief of Staff. *Epitome of the Russo-Japanese War* (Washington: Government Printing Office, 1906), 42; Smith places the number of attackers at 120,000, which seams high considering the total force in July 1904 was 65,000. The only substantial addition to this force recorded was the 20,000-man, 9th Division arriving in November. Giannitrappani gives a more realistic number in his account as 90,000." Kuhn, one of the U.S. Observers with Nogi places the number at 80,000. Giannitrappani, "The Operations Round Port Arthur in 1904. Three Lectures by Captain L. Giannitrappani of the Italian Artillery," 259; Kuhn, 801; Smith, 476; and Anderson, 93; Thuiller states the number was "nearly 100,000." Thuillier, 68

[202] Most accounts agree that the Russians surrendered between 41,000 and 44,000 men. Ginnitrappani states the total Russian prisoners were given as 41,600, including 17 flag officers. A total of 26,000 Russians were listed as killed in action during the defense. The Official Russian account places the total on hand strength on January 2nd as 38,858. Giannitrappani, "The Operations Around Port Arthur in the Year 1904, The Development of the Investment and Siege of the Fortress," 384; Thuillier, 67; and Tettau, part 2, 502; Larry Addington, in his book placed the total losses at 65,000. Larry Addington, *The Patterns of War Since the Eighteenth Century,* 2d ed. (Bloomington: Indiana University Press, 1994), 131.

[203] Thuillier, 60; Fuller, 141; Beasley, 72-74; W. B. (pseudonym), "Reflections on Russian Strategy in Manchuria in 1904," *The Journal of the United Service Institution of India* 159 (April 1905): 175-176.

[204] Giannitrappani, "The Operations Round Port Arthur in 1904. Three Lectures by Captain L. Giannitrappani of the Italian Artillery," 259.

[205] "Precis of Foreign Military Papers, Russian Papers," *The Journal of the United Service Institution of India* 175 (April 1909): 249-250; Ruckman, 3.

[206] "Precis of Foreign Military Papers, Russian Papers," *The Journal of the United Service Institution of India* 175, 250; Fuller, 143.

CHAPTER 3

THE BATTLE OF MUKDEN

The aim of this battle is to decide the fate of the war, so it is not a question of occupying certain points or taking tracks of land.[1]

Marshal Oyama, Directive to the Japanese Manchurian Army at Mukden

This chapter will look at The Battle of Mukden, the final major land battle of the Russo-Japanese War. The Battle of Mukden was distinctly different from the Siege of Port Arthur. While the Port Arthur siege demonstrated modern weapons in a somewhat stationary battle, the Battle of Mukden featured large-scale large maneuver warfare, with corps and army movements. The Battle of Mukden was the largest battle fought in the Russo-Japanese War and was the largest battle fought in history up to that point.[2] Over 600,000 combatants fought on a front extending ninety miles.[3] To control these large armies, both the Japanese and Russian commanders used the telegraph and telephone extensively. In addition to new communications systems, every modern weapon system of the time was represented and the latest maneuver tactics were tested.[4]

Military and civilian observers recorded the events of the sixteen-day Battle of Mukden in the same voluminous fashion that they recorded the Port Arthur siege. These observer accounts illustrate the lethal combined effects of the hand grenade, machinegun, improvised trench mortar, and field artillery on the 20th Century battlefield.

The following narrative will use the international observer accounts of the Battle of Mukden to illustrate what lessons were available to the observer nations in the period just prior to the beginning of the First World War. These accounts clearly illustrate that the lethality of modern weapons found at Port Arthur was not an exception but by 1904, a reality in modern combat.

The Armies that Fought at Mukden

Both the Japanese and Russian governments chose their best military leaders to execute the Russo-Japanese War and both were present as commanders at Mukden. To command the Japanese forces, Marshal Iwao Oyama, the prewar Japanese Army Chief of Staff, was selected. The son of a Samurai, Marshal Oyama joined the army as it began modernizing in the 1860s. In 1870, Marshal Oyama was selected to go to Europe as an observer of the Franco-Prussian War. In 1884, he returned to Europe to request German instructors to teach German drill and regulations at Japanese military colleges.[5] During the Sino-Japanese War, Oyama served as an army commander and was an obvious choice to command the Japanese Manchurian Army.[6] To defeat the Russian Manchurian Army quickly and set the conditions for a favorable negotiated peace, Marshal Oyama desired to execute a large-scale envelopment, similar to the German success at Sedan in 1870, somewhere in Manchuria.[7]

While the Japanese leadership used German staff models for its organization, the Japanese military manpower system was also based on the German example. Prior to the war, 40,000--50,000 soldiers were conscripted into the Japanese Army each year for a three-year period. At the completion of this active duty, these troops served an additional four years and four months in the active or First Reserve, which was used to bring active divisions to full strength in times of war. At the end of this term, the soldiers would enter the inactive or Second Reserve for another five-year period.[8] At the beginning of the war,

Japan had an active force of 200,000 soldiers and a trained reserve force of over 300,000. Additionally, there were another 200,000 draft age men available for service.[9]

To execute the war, Japan mobilized its divisions over several months, with the last pre-war divisions arriving in Manchuria in September 1904. Beginning in September, Japan also activated soldiers from its inactive or Second Reserve to replace mounting front line casualties. Using activated Second and First Reserves, Japan maintained its front line divisions at 100 percent strength throughout the war.[10] To replace officer casualties, Japan commissioned officer cadets from its military academies earlier than their scheduled graduations.[11] Throughout the war, Japan maintained combat units at their authorized levels, with replacements often being assigned within days of reported losses.[12]

The Japanese infantry drill regulation, published before the war, used many of the concepts developed in Germany.[13] The Japanese believed that in an infantry versus infantry battle, the victor owed his success to the use of superior marksmanship, firepower, discipline, and control.[14] To enhance marksmanship training, the Japanese conducted ranges with soldiers under "battle conditions," wearing full marching gear.[15] In addition to precision marksmanship, Japan considered firepower a prerequisite to enable infantry to get close enough to the enemy to "charge with the bayonet."[16] The integration of massed firepower seen at Port Arthur was repeated at The Battle of Mukden.

Japanese tactics did change after the early battles In Manchuria. By the end of July 1904, the Japanese adopted an extended formation, with officers and non-commissioned officers using whistles to control fifteen to twenty man sections as they advanced in rushes. During these advances, one section fired while the other section advanced.[17] While several of the observer accounts claim this formation was new, it was in fact cited as a form of maneuver in Japan's prewar infantry drill regulation.[18] After experiencing the heavy losses of the war's first battles, Japan adopted extended formations as its primary form of infantry maneuver. To defend against the massed firepower of Russians in the defense, the Japanese began to dig hasty defensive positions whenever halted, even during lulls in an attack.[19] In attacks over the frozen featureless ground of Mukden, the Japanese infantry improvised a new type of cover during attacks. To provide protection from Russian direct fire after conducting a rush, Japanese infantry began carrying bags filled with earth and sand forward in the advance. At the completion of a rush, they placed the bags to their front as a firing platform and for protection.[20] During the battles around Mukden, this technique was used extensively to overcome the effects of the frozen earth.[21] To blend in with the surrounding terrain, Japanese uniform color was modified from blue to khaki. Thus, during one Japanese attack at Mukden, a Russian infantryman stated that the Japanese "vanished" at the end of a rush due to the color of their uniforms and excellent use of terrain.[22]

After the fall of Port Arthur, Japanese engineers that were stripped from the Manchurian Armies in September 1904 were reassigned to their parent divisions. As these troops returned to their original units, they quickly spread the combat lessons learned at Port Arthur, especially the use of the hand grenades and trench mortars.[23]

By the beginning of 1905, the Japanese Army desired to conduct what it hoped would be the final decisive battle. In the north, Marshal Oyama commanded three armies (the First, Second, and Fourth), with nine full strength divisions and several reserve brigades.[24] On 18 January, after the capture of Port Arthur, the Third Army, with its four divisions, began marching north to join the remainder of the Manchurian Army. The artillery of the Army was moved north by rail. The Third Army arrived at Liao-Yang in mid-February.[25]

The commander of Russia's Manchurian Army was General Alexei Kuropatkin. General Kuropatkin was born in 1848 to a noble family. He graduated first in his class from the Nicholas Military Academy in 1874, and served as a division chief of staff in the 1877-1878 Russo-Turkish War.[26] Kuropatkin was made a general officer at age thirty-six and was considered in Russia to be a soldier-scholar, studying the military art and publishing military works.[27] In 1898, Kuropatkin was appointed as Russia's Minister of War and on 20 February 1904, he was selected to command Russia's Manchurian Army.[28]

While considered an extremely capable and intelligent man in Europe and Russia, General Kuropatkin's actions in the field would reveal several character weaknesses. General Kuropatkin was prone to hesitation and slow to make decisions on the battlefield.[29] The Japanese had a more accurate picture of Kuropatkin, and held him in very low esteem, stating that he "never attempts any great movement, but is always content with nibbling and retiring."[30]

While it appeared that Russia was caught unprepared to fight a war with Japan, General Kuropatkin, as the Russian War Minister, had ordered an extensive study for a Far East campaign. In 1903, after a visit to Manchuria and Japan, he established the "General Principles of Operations against Japan."[31] Under these principles, he planned to trade land for time to build up Russian forces to defeat the Japanese.[32] His plan allowed

Japan to occupy Korea and then move north into Manchuria. Russian forces were to avoid decisive engagements and offer only limited resistance to slow the Japanese advance until Russian strength grew. In this study, Kuropatkin determined that the Russian Far East Fleet was critical to defeating troop landings. With no interference, Kuropatkin estimated that Japan could land three divisions in Korea within three weeks of declaring war and another three divisions a week later. He expected the Japanese to maintain the initiative during the first two months of the war, but after six months, he expected the advantage to shift to Russia.[33] Once Russia built up sufficient strength, its army would drive the Japanese out of Manchuria and Korea, and eventually invade Japan.[34] General Kuropatkin's estimation of Japan's capabilities and timeline proved very accurate, but he greatly overestimated Russia's ability to gain the initiative. The overall plan to give ground to gain time for reinforcements to arrive was sound, but Russia's Army never escaped the mental attitude of a passive defense during the war.[35] The Japanese, on the other hand, seized and kept the initiative throughout the war.[36]

At the beginning of the war Russia had the largest standing army in the world, with an active force of 1,100,000 soldiers. This army, however, was almost solely focused on the threat of a European war, and during the first year of the Russo-Japanese War, no active European corps or divisions were committed to Manchuria.[37] During this period, Russia attempted to fight a limited war, committing the smallest forces perceived necessary to defeat Japan. It was not until mid-1905, after the Battle of Mukden, that the first active units were deployed from European Russia to Manchuria.[38]

The Russian Army that fought at Mukden was significantly different from the active divisions that fought at Port Arthur. In February 1904, the Russian Manchurian

Army numbered approximately 150,000 men.[39] By September 1904, this number was increased by 170,000 troops, including troops from seven newly mobilized reserve divisions.[40] These divisions were built around an active cadre or "skeleton" field organization of about 25 percent active troops.[41] The leadership for these units was drawn from existing cadre, with brigade headquarters staffs that were expanded into division staffs and battalion staffs that were expanded into brigade and regimental staffs.[42]

To ensure that Russia could mobilize troops for a European contingency, Russia only mobilized its less-capable Second Class Reserves.[43] In an average 220-man reserve division company, up to 160 soldiers came from the second reserve.[44] By comparison, an active division maintained a cadre of roughly 114 soldiers and, during mobilization, would be filled to 100 percent with First Class Reserves, who had only recently been released from active service.[45] By mobilizing only older, Second Class Reserves, Russia began the war with a significant disadvantage to the front line Japanese divisions they would face.

Training the newly mobilized soldiers also posed a problem for the Russian Army. To reduce the costs of the war, the Russian Government staggered the mobilization of its units to fit the rail deployment timeline. This desire to save all possible costs for this "limited war," resulted in almost no train-up of mobilized forces.[46] Most of the mobilized troops received as little as ten days training before making the forty to fifty day train movement to Manchuria. During the first year of the war, these newly mobilized troops often went into battle immediately upon arriving in Manchuria.[47] While most of the activated soldiers had previous army service, some had never seen the Model 1891 rifle, introduced thirteen years prior.[48] Little was done to familiarize these soldiers with their basic weapon, as the Russian marksmanship regulation allotted only twenty qualification rounds for mobilized troops. New recruits, in comparision, were allotted 125 rounds for annual range training.[49] The prewar Russian range training manual also failed to address the improved range and accuracy of the new rifle, with half of the 125 rounds used for volley firing drills.[50] Not only were the Russian divisions manned with older soldiers than the standard Japanese division, they also received much less training than the activated Japanese soldiers.

In 1904, Russian infantry tactics still followed 19th Century lines, and had not progressed to match the capabilities of modern weapons.[51] To counter field artillery effects, troops were trained to move in files with a ten-pace interval. When under fire, soldiers were to run while "stooping," and use terrain for cover when possible.[52] In the attack, Russian tactics called for the use of shock effect. Troops were to fire one rifle volley at the enemy followed by a bayonet charge.[53] No combined training of newly mobilized infantry and artillery units was conducted prior to their deployment to Manchuria.[54]

The lack of individual and section training also negated the advantage that the new Model 1900 quick-fire artillery piece gave the Russians. Many of the gunners received their only instruction on the weapon in the rail cars en route to Manchuria and did not fire the system until they were in combat with the Japanese.[55] It was only in the last months of 1904 and early months of 1905 that arriving units were able to conduct limited combined arms training.[56] Due to this limited integrated training, Russian artillery failed to effectively support Russian infantry in the defense or during counterattacks during the Mukden battle.[57]

Events leading up to The Battle of Mukden

In the period between the Battle of the Yalu and the surrender of Port Arthur in January 1905, the Japanese and Russians fought several major and minor battles in Manchuria. The three major land battles that took place during this period were the Battle of Wa-Fang-Gou in June 1904, the Battle of Liao-Yang in June and July 1904, and the Battle of Sha-ho in October 1904.[58]

While none of these battles were decisive for either side, each encounter ended with a Russian withdrawal that left the Japanese in control of the battlefield. During these battles, Japan was forced to commit its reserves to secure a tactical victory and was then unable to exploit the retreat of the Russian forces with a strong pursuit. The inconclusive Battle of Sha Ho in October 1904 left both the Russian and Japanese forces exhausted.[59] After this battle, both armies dug in along the Sha Ho River to reorganize. The Russian's assumed defensive positions to await additional reinforcements from Russia, while the Japanese assumed a defensive posture to await the arrival of the Third Army, as the fall of Port Arthur was expected at any time.[60] As the Battle of Mukden began, the Russian forces had occupied the same terrain for almost five months.

After the fall of Port Arthur, General Kuropatkin attempted to interdict the movement of the Japanese Third Army to the north with the war's largest cavalry raid.[61] Beginning on 8 January, over 8,000 cavalry troops moved south to conduct attacks on Japanese railroad and telegraph sites.[62] During the ten-day raid, Russian cavalry traveled 180 miles and conducted several decentralized attacks on railroad and telegraph stations in the Japanese rear area. Overall, the raid was considered unsuccessful, as it failed to destroy any railroad bridges or inflict any lasting damage.[63]

On 19 January, prior to the arrival of the Japanese Third Army, General Kuropatkin decided to exploit his current numerical advantage and conduct an attack on the Japanese near the town of San-De-Pu.[64] The attack commenced on 25 January, against the western flank of the Japanese, with the goal of cutting off the Japanese lines of communication to the south.[65] While Kuropatkin intended the offensive to exploit his numerical superiority over the Japanese, he committed less than half of his available troops, keeping two full corps as a reserve.[66] The Japanese, defended from the numerous villages they had occupied for the winter and committed all of their available reserves to halt the Russian attack. By 27 January, the Japanese halted the Russian attack and launched a counterattack. On 31 January, the Russian ground commander ended the seven-day battle and ordered a retreat to his initial positions.[67]

The Russians were defeated by several factors, including Kuropatkin's indecisiveness and failure to commit a larger portion of his available forces. The weather was also a major factor, as it remained between ten and twenty degrees below freezing in the daytime hours.[68] The battle ended with the Russians losing 12,000-15,000 casualties and the Japanese losing 10,000. Both armies suffered significant casualties from frostbite.[69] Had the Russian attack been successful in cutting the Japanese lines of communications, the course of the Battle of Mukden could have changed significantly or been postponed.[70]

As the Battle of San-De-Pu was ending, the Japanese launched a cavalry raid into northern Manchuria to disrupt Russian lines of communication. On 11 February, a Japanese force, numbering only 150 troops, conducted a raid 160 miles north of Mukden.[71] These raiders destroyed a bridge on the Hsinkai Ho River, stopping rail traffic to the south for two weeks.[72] A secondary and more important effect of this raid was its impact on General Kuropatkin. To counter the threat of future attacks on his lines of communication, he committed over 40,000 additional troops, and a large portion of his cavalry force to guard the rail line north of Mukden.[73] By assigning a large cavalry screening force to his rear area, General Kuropatkin effectively stripped away much of his mobile reconnaissance and intelligence force from supporting him at Mukden.

The Terrain and Plans of Attack at Mukden

In 1905, the city of Mukden was the largest city in Manchuria, with a population of 200,000 people. Located along the Hun-Ho River some 260 miles northeast of Port Arthur, it was the traditional home of the reigning dynasties of China. The Manchurian branch of the Trans-Siberian Railroad ran two miles to the west of Mukden.[74] The terrain to the west of the city was a relatively open plain, dotted with numerous villages containing mud and brick buildings.[75] The terrain south and north of Mukden consisted of rolling hills that were broken by the Hun-Ho and Sha-Ho Rivers. To the east, the rolling hills quickly rose into mountainous terrain. The Hun-Ho River begins in the mountains to the northeast of Mukden and flows to the southwest, two miles south of the city. The Sha-Ho River follows a similar course twelve to fifteen miles south of Mukden and then enters into the Tai-Tsu-Ho River, which parallels the Hun-Ho River. During the winter months, both the rivers and the ground were frozen solid. While the frozen rivers allowed the Japanese to easily cross the water obstacles, the frozen plowed fields slowed foot movement due to the rough footing caused by the furrows.[76]

The arrival of the four divisions of the Third Army at Liao-Yang allowed Marshal Oyama to begin maneuvering his forces for the planned decisive battle. Liao-Yang, located 37 miles south of Mukden, was Japan's primary supply base in northern Manchuria and all Japanese armies were located north of the town. In addition to the arrival of the Third Army, several Kobi (reserve) brigades arrived in Manchuria to strengthen the Japanese force.[77] With these additional forces, Marshall Oyama formed the Japanese Fifth Army by assigning to it the 11th Division from the Third Army and by forming a Kobi division using two Kobi brigades. The Fifth Army had an additional Kobi brigade as its reserve. The Japanese general reserve consisted of the 3rd Division and two Kobi brigades.[78]

Operating with five armies, Marshal Oyama planned a large double envelopment of Mukden, with the main effort in the west, and a supporting attack in the east.[79] The order for the attack was issued on 20 February, with the eastern attack to begin on 23 February. The attack in the west was to commence several days later, with the hope that Russia would misread the Japanese main effort.[80] Marshal Oyama planned to envelop the Russians at Mukden, force a retreat, and then destroy the Russian Army as it retreated.[81]

In the west, the main effort of the Japanese attack was to move north of the Hun-Ho River and attack Mukden from the east and rear. This mission was given to the Third Army, now consisting of three divisions and one Kobi brigade as its reserve.[82] In order to hide the whereabouts of the Third Army, it was positioned behind the Japanese Second Army on the eastern flank. The Third Army was to remain stationary for several days after the initial attacks and then begin a flanking movement to the east of Mukden.[83] The

Third Army's cavalry brigade was augmented with infantry and was to screen the army's advance.[84]

To conduct the supporting attack in the east, Marshal Oyama used the Fifth Army. This decision greatly benefited the Japanese plan of attack, as the Russians identified the 11th Division early in the battle and then assumed that the entire Third Army was operating in the east as the Japanese main effort.[85]

The remaining three Japanese armies were arrayed to the east of the Fifth Army. The First Japanese Army with two divisions and three Kobi brigades was located directly to the west of the Fifth Army. Next to the First Army was the Fourth Army with two divisions and two Kobi brigades. On the western flank was the Second Army, which contained three divisions and two Kobi brigades. The Second Army was to keep all forces to its front tied down, to secure the movement of the Third Army into its flanking movement.[86] The Second Army would directly support the main effort later in the battle as it pivoted to the northeast to maintain contact with the Third Army's flank during its movement. The overall mission of the center armies was to hold the Russian Armies in place until the two flanking armies arrived at the rear of Mukden. In reserve, Marshal Oyama maintained the 3rd division and three Kobi brigades.[87]

To support this force of almost 325,000 soldiers, the Japanese employed over 900 field guns and 170 heavy guns, including several of the heavy 11-inch guns, which were moved north from Port Arthur by rail. The Japanese force also had 200 machineguns that were used in the attack.[88]

Command and control of this massive infantry and artillery force was one of the smallest challenges encountered by the Japanese leadership. After the Battle of Sha-Ho in

October 1904, the armies of Japan used the telephone heavily for all tactical reporting (versus the traditional use of runners).[89] Telegraph and telephone wire connected all division and brigade headquarters, and often went down to battalion level.[90] As units moved, Japanese signal troops rolled out communications wire to maintain communications with its higher headquarters.[91] As at Port Arthur, all artillery batteries were connected by telephone to control their fires.[92] During the flanking movements of Third Army, artillery officers moved forward with the attacks and sent fire support requests by telephone to supporting artillery battalions.[93] Throughout the battle, Marshal Oyama was able to remain stationary in his headquarters and receive reports and issue orders almost instantaneously.[94]

As the Japanese began developing their attack plans, the Russian Manchurian Army continued to grow with the daily arrival of new troops and equipment by rail. By mid-February 1905, General Kuropatkin controlled three armies and a large general reserve. These forces were placed in defensive positions south of Mukden. The Second Russian Army, consisting of three corps, was stationed in the west. The Third Russian Army, with three corps, defended due south of Mukden along the Sha-Ho River. The First Russian Army with four corps was positioned in the east, in the mountainous region. To secure the flanks of the Russian Army, Kuropatkin positioned forces on each flank. In the east, two infantry divisions and three cavalry regiments secured the flank of the First Army. In the west, one and a half cavalry divisions and an infantry brigade were deployed to protect the flank of the Second Army. General Kuropatkin's reserve consisted of a reinforced corps located near Mukden.[95] The total Russian force was relatively equal to that of Japan, totaling approximately 325,000 men. These troops were supported by 1,200 artillery pieces (including 250 heavy artillery pieces) and 88 machine guns.[96]

Since the Battle of the Sha-Ho in October, the Russian forces had remained relatively stationary and had continuously improved their defensive positions around Mukden. Two defensive lines were built, one paralleling the Sha-Ho River and a second constructed on the outskirts of Mukden. The southern defensive line was the strongest and consisted of well-dug fortifications, with numerous strong points and a multi-tiered trench systems. These fortifications were surrounded by wire with integrated automatic and electrically detonated mines. In some many cases, the mud buildings that dotted the countryside were integrated into the defenses. To support these various defensive lines, ammunition magazines and supply points were positioned near the front.[97] Many of the defending units were connected by telephone communications at the brigade and division level, but communications to General Kuropatkin's headquarters was limited.[98] Russian and Japanese defensive lines remained separated by about four to five miles after the San-De-Pu battle.[99]

The Battle of Mukden, 19 February to 01 March 1905

As Marshal Oyama began maneuvering his forces for the attack, General Kuropatkin was planning an offensive of his own. His plan, issued on 19 February, was nearly a repeat of the failed January attack at San-De-Pu. The decision to repeat the January attack was based on his belief that the plan itself was solid and only failed due to the poor leadership of the ground commander.[100] The attack was to commence on 23 February, with an attack against the Japanese western flank.[101]

On 19 February, the day General Kuropatkin issued his offensive order, the Japanese Fifth Army began moving through the mountainous terrain in the east in two columns. The Japanese came into contact earlier than expected, when they ran into dug in elements of the Russian eastern flank detachment on the first day of their advance.[102] The Russians occupied naturally defensible terrain with integrated machineguns. The attacks initially stalled, until the Japanese began attacking using coordinated fires of mountain guns, machineguns and hand grenades. Using this focused firepower, the Japanese quickly resumed its offensive and forced the Russians from their positions.[103] During these close attacks, the soldiers of the Japanese 11th Division announced to the defenders, that they had come from Port Arthur to defeat them. This information was quickly reported up the Russian chain of command, where it was then assumed that the entire Third Army was fighting in the East.[104]

General Kuropatkin, soon began to waver in his plans to attack the Japanese western flank, and postponed his planned attack.[105] By 24 February, General Kuropatkin believed the Japanese were committing their main effort in the east and cancelled the attack all together. To defend against what he believed was the main Japanese attack, Kuropatkin ordered two brigades from his reserve to deploy 40 miles east to support the defenders. On 25 February, Kuropatkin ordered the 1st Siberian Corps, then attached to the Russian Second Army, to march east as well, significantly reducing his combat power in the west.[106] From 25 to 28 February, the Fifth Army advanced fifteen miles in the mountainous terrain with temperatures falling to negative twenty-two degrees at night. The Fifth Army's attacks finally stalled on 28 February, when the Russian defenses were finally strong enough to halt the Japanese advance.[107]

On 26 February, the Japanese First and Fourth Armies began artillery attacks on the Russian lines and conducted limited maneuver attacks. Both armies were to hold the Russian forces to their front in place, while the mission of the First Army was to also draw Russian forces away from the Fifth Army's advance in the east. For six days, the two armies made artillery attacks and limited ground assaults to hold the Russians in place. The Fourth Army remained stationary during the first days of the battle, using artillery fire to keep the Russian defenders from redeploying.[108] On the night of 27 February, the Russians launched a limited ground attack against the Japanese Fourth Army across the Sha Ho River. While the Russians had initial success, the Japanese later counterattacked and regained all lost ground.[109]

The mission of the Second Army, to the east of the Fourth Army, was different from the tasks assigned to the other central armies. While its primary mission was to hold the Russian forces to its front in place, the Second Army was also responsible for maintaining contact with the Japanese Third Army as it moved to the east. From 27 to 29 February, the Second Army launched artillery attacks on the Russian lines to cover the initial movement of the Third Army.[110] On 1 March, the Second Army began offensive operations to maintain contact with the Third Army on its left. By this date, the Third Army had advanced over thirty miles to the north, and was beginning to open a gap between its divisions and those of the Second Army.[111] During the initial two days of its attacks, the Second Army's western divisions advanced ten miles against strong Russian defenses.[112]

The main effort of the Japanese attack, the Third Army, began movement on 27 February, from its position five to ten miles to the rear of the Second Army. The Third

Army advanced in four columns, with its cavalry brigade screening the move to the north and west. Russian cavalry, screening the western flank of the Russian lines, identified the Japanese movement on the first day of the advance and reported it to their headquarters. On the following day, additional reports were sent to the Russian Second Army Headquarters reporting that one or two Japanese divisions were moving. The Russian leadership ordered additional surveillance of this movement, but overall, did nothing to stop the movement, allowing the Japanese Third Army almost unhindered progress for several more days.[113] During the Third Army's march, only the 9th Division, the southern anchor of the four columns, entered into any major contact. While the 9th Division remained in contact, the 1st Division in the north and the 7th Division in the middle continued to move north. By the end of 2 March, the Third Army had traveled over seventy-five kilometers toward the Russian rear area.[114]

As the Japanese attacks began across his front, General Kuropatkin had trouble gaining a clear picture of the situation. The strength of the artillery fires to his center and reports of the massing of forces in the west forced Kuropatkin to reevaluate his decision to send additional forces to the east. On 27 February, Kuropatkin ordered the 1st Siberian Corps to return to the western flank from the east, where it had just arrived from his 25 February move.[115] The 1st Siberian Corps arrived in the west on 2 March, after the countermarch order, traveling ninety miles in seven days without any enemy contact.[116]

On 28 February, Kuropatkin ordered the 25th Division from his general reserve, to move to the west to reinforce the Second Russian Army against the attacks of the Japanese Second and Third Armies.[117] On the same day, he also ordered a brigade size element from his reserve to move north of Mukden as additional security for the railroad.[118] By 1 March, General Kuropatkin was sure that the Third Army was focused on flanking his army, and he began planning a counterattack against the Japanese advances.[119]

The Battle of Mukden, 2 March to 7 March 1905

During this phase of the battle, Marshal Oyama transferred forces from the Second Army to the Third Army and committed his reserve to the attack. On 2 March, the cavalry brigade of Second Army was assigned to support Third Army's cavalry screening to the north.[120] On 3 March, the 8th Division was taken from the Second Army and sent to the Third Army to strengthen the flanking movement.[121] On 4 March, Marshal Oyama released the 3rd Division from his reserve to fill the area vacated by the 8th Division.[122] The last of Oyama's reserves were committed on 6 March, when his remaining two Kobi brigades were assigned to the Third Army to exploit the army's success.[123]

In the east, the Japanese Fifth Army met stiff resistance from the Russian First Army and was unable to advance from their 28 February positions. Even with the withdrawal of the 1st Siberian Corps, the Russian commander had four available corps to defend against the attacks of two Japanese divisions. The Russians, fighting from dug in positions, used machineguns, artillery, and hand grenades to stop the Japanese attacks. On 1 March, during a coordinated Japanese attack, the Russian defenders inflicted over 1,000 casualties on the Japanese with a loss of 500 Russian casualties.[124] The Russian defenders would hold the Japanese from gaining further ground in the east until March 8th, when Kuropatkin ordered a retreat of all Russian forces back to Mukden.[125]

On 1 March, the Japanese First and Fourth Armies began ground attacks against what was considered the strongest portion of the Russian defenses at Mukden. In the months after the Battle of Sha-Ho, the Russians had dug several lines of trenches that were surrounded by wire and had integrated machineguns. These trenches were connected by telephone and had communication with supporting artillery batteries.[126] On 2 March, elements of the Japanese 10th Division (Fourth Army) launched an attack against Putilov Hill located on the hills overlooking the frozen Sha-Ho River.[127] To support the brigade size attack, the Japanese concentrated the direct fires of machineguns and three batteries of mountain guns in direct support, as well as indirect fires that included support from several 11-inch guns.[128] To get to Putilov Hill, the Japanese had to cover 600 meters of open ground. During the attack, the Japanese infantry carried their mobile cover of sandbags as they advanced forward by rushes.[129] Using this cumbersome protection, the Japanese infantry successfully seized the first trench line in front of the Putilov Hill defenses. After achieving this line, however, the Russians concentrated all available fire on the area to the stop any reinforcement of the brigade. For several days, the Japanese attempted to continue their attack, but were defeated each time by concentrated Russian fires from strong defensive positions.[130] Only on 8 March, after the defenders were ordered to fall back to Mukden, did the advance continue.[131]

On 5 March, the Japanese 6th Division of the Fourth Army launched an attack to close a gap between its left flank and that of the advancing Second Army. In the attack, the Japanese advanced four to five miles and then dug in along a new line where it remained until the 8 March Russian withdrawal.[132]

The Japanese First Army continued artillery and limited ground attacks on the Russian defenses until 4 March, when it was ordered to attack to the east and support the stalled advance of the Fifth Army. The attack was launched on 5 March and, over the next two days, advanced seven miles into the flank and rear of the Russian defenders.[133] Early on 7 March, the First Army repulsed a Russian counterattack that attempted to pierce the Japanese defenses along the Sha-Ho River.[134] The defeat of this counterattack and the later defeat of a major counterattack in the east influenced General Kuropatkin in ordering a general retreat of his forces back to Mukden on the night of 7 March.

From 2 to 7 March, the Japanese Second Army advanced twelve to fifteen miles to stay in contact with the Third Army's flanking movement. During this advance, the army used the combined effects of massed firepower in its attacks. As at Port Arthur, the Japanese brought machineguns and artillery forward to provide direct fire support to the attacking infantry. In one attack, the direct fires of twelve mountain guns supported a battalion and a half of infantry as it advanced. In another attack, thirty-six mountain guns provided direct fires to support the attack of a Japanese infantry regiment. The larger guns of the regular artillery batteries were also consistently moved forward, to support the attacks.[135] In addition to these larger munitions, the Second Army used hand grenades and trench mortars to increase the firepower used against the Russian defenders.[136] To provide cover from Russian direct fires in the near featureless terrain, the Japanese Second Army also used the sand filled bags to provide protection as they advanced in rushes. Using these tactics, the Japanese Second Army was able to continue their advance against the Russian defenses.[137]

While generally successful, the Russian's did inflict substantial losses on the Japanese in many of their attacks. In one extremely costly engagement to seize a village in a defensive line, the Japanese were defeated by a coordinated Russian effort.[138] On 7 March, a brigade from the 3rd Division attacked a Russian defensive position that was integrated into the village of Yu-Haun-Tun. The Japanese initial attack was successful and, by 11:00 A.M., the Japanese were in control of the village. Almost immediately, however, the Russian's began a series of counterattacks. During these counterattacks, both sides used hand grenades and trench mortars in house to house fighting.[139] The Russians also employed four artillery pieces in a direct fire role to dislodge the Japanese. At nightfall, after twelve hours of continuous fighting, the Japanese brigade commander ordered a withdrawal from the village. The attack and later defense of the village cost the Japanese 4,200 men killed and wounded from its committed 5,500-man brigade. The Russians lost 5,400 casualties in their attacks.[140] On 8 March, after the hard won battle was over, the Russians evacuated the village as the withdrawal to Mukden was ordered.

The first major contact experienced by the Japanese Third Army took place on 2 March, when two Russian divisions conducted a counterattack against the flank of the advancing Japanese forces.[141] The Japanese 1st and 7th Divisions defeated the counterattack, but both divisions took heavy casualties. The size and aggressiveness of the Russian attack made General Nogi, the commander of the Third Army, decide to slow his northern advance in order to concentrate his forces.[142] The Russian force repeated the failed attack on the following day, and after its second defeat, withdrew to the east.[143]

On 4 March, Marshal Oyama ordered the Third Army (then due west of Mukden) to move further north and not to become tied up in fighting around the city of Mukden.[144]

On 5 March, the Third Army began redistributing its forces, ordering the 1st Division further north, and order the southern most division (the 9th Division) to move into the gap formed by the 1st Division's advance. The 8th Division, now assigned to First Army, was ordered to move north and fill the hole in the lines created by moving 9th Division. As this difficult maneuver began, the Russians launched an attack against the Third Army.

General Kuropatkin ordered a counterattack against the flank of the Third Army on 5 March after he realized the threat that Nogi's army now posed to his lines of communication.[145] To conduct the attack, Kuropatkin ordered the establishment of a composite element of units from three corps in the Russian Second Army.[146] At this point in the battle, Russian forces in the west outnumbered the Japanese 120,000 to 100,000. The commander of the Second Army, however, committed only 33 of an available 110 battalions to the attack.[147]

After a long artillery bombardment, the attack began at 11:00 A.M. on 6 March. The attack was focused on a portion of the Japanese line that was recently vacated by the Japanese 1st Division as it moved north. To oppose the Russian attack was only one battalion of the 7th Division, which had extended its line to the north while awaiting the arrival of the 9th Division. The Russian attack was a half-hearted effort at best, while the Japanese, though significantly outnumbered, they were supported by strong artillery. The small defensive force was able to hold the line long enough for the 9th Division to arrive. By 3:00 P.M., the Russian Second Army Commander called off the attack and ordered his troop back to their starting point.[148] The Russian commander had failed to seize the opportunity to defeat the Japanese flanking force by using overwhelming force at a decisive point in the battle. From this point forward, the Russian armies would remain on a defensive footing until their final withdrawal to the north.

The Battle of Mukden, 8 March to 10 March 1905

Soon after the counterattack against the Third Army failed, General Kuropatkin received a report of a cavalry raid (conducted by the Third Army's Cavalry Division) on a railroad station north of Mukden. These two events resulted in General Kuropatkin ordering a retreat of all Russian forces back to the Hun-Ho River.[149] At 3:00 A.M. on March 8th, Kuropatkin issued an order for the withdrawal of all his forces. To cover this withdrawal, he ordered the creation of a forty-battalion general reserve from the armies as they withdrew.[150]

As the Russian forces prepared to withdraw, they began burning forward storehouses and magazines. The smoke from behind the Russian lines alerted the Japanese of their intentions, and Marshal Oyama ordered a general attack across the entire front.[151] In addition to ordering the attack, Marshall Oyama also ordered the Third Army to speed its movements to the north to cut off the Russian escape route. The Japanese commander assumed that the Russians were retreating north of Mukden and did not realize that General Kuropatkin only planned to withdraw to Mukden.[152]

General Kuropatkin's intent for this withdrawal to the Hun-Ho River was to shorten his defensive lines, with the goal of later conducting a counterattack.[153] His plans were soon circumvented, however, by the initiative of the Japanese. In the east, the Russian First Army conducted a coordinated withdrawal and arrived on the Hun-Ho ready to fight. In the center, however, the withdrawal was very disorganized. When the

Japanese First and Fourth Army's began its full pursuit, the Russian forces in the center were unable to slow their advance, and by 9 March, the Japanese were across the frozen Hun-Ho River and had penetrated the Russian defensive lines.[154] The penetration of the defenses at the Hun-Ho River and the threat of being cut off by the Third Army resulted in Kuropatkin's decision to end all offensive plans. On the evening of 9 March he ordered a general retreat from Mukden.[155]

While the Russian's failed to execute either a good offensive or defensive operation at Mukden, they were able to conduct a fighting withdrawal, and were able to save two-thirds of their fighting force.[156] In the north, the Japanese Third Army was unable to completely cut off the Russian retreat, but was able to close within artillery range and began firing artillery rounds at the retreating Russians beginning on 10 March.[157] The Russian force initially withdrew to Tiehling forty miles to the north of Mukden, arriving on 13 March. On 16 March, General Kuropatkin ordered a retreat further north to His-ping-Kai, where the Russian forces dug in for the remainder of the war.[158]

When the Russians began their retreat, the Japan could not exploit the situation. After sixteen-days of continuous battle, the Japanese troops were too exhausted to pursue. To ensure success, Marshal Oyama had committed his reserves early in the battle to exploit the success of the Third Army.[159] As the Russians retreated, the Japanese commander was able to commit only two divisions to the pursuit.[160]

During the battle, Russia lost 96,500 men, approximately one third of its original force. These numbers include 19,000 prisoners and 14,000 killed.[161] While the Russians lost vast amounts of supplies when they evacuated Mukden, they lost only fifty-eight of their 1,200 artillery pieces. This small number would normally indicate a skilled withdrawal. In fact, General Kuropatkin, in fear of being defeated, ordered the first of his heavy artillery and supporting trains out of Mukden on 6 March, the day before his failed March 7th counterattack.[162]

Initial Japanese losses were reported as 41,000 men, one eighth of its attacking force at Mukden.[163] After the war, this number was increased to 71,000 or twenty-two percent of its attacking force.[164] The Japanese Second Army took the greatest number of casualties, losing 22,000 men in its frontal assaults against the Russian right wing. The Third Army experienced the second greatest number of casualties, losing 18,000 soldiers as it defeated the 6 and 7 March counterattacks.[165]

Summary

The observer accounts of the Battle of Mukden clearly illustrate that the lethality of weapons used at Port Arthur was not an anomaly of that one battle. These same weapons were used again at Mukden to provide decisive firepower at critical points in the battle. During the battle, both the defender and the attacker used machineguns, hand grenades, mortars, and artillery to support maneuver. The Japanese continued to focus on using massed firepower to critical points in the battle. The effectiveness of the machinegun in the attack was again illustrated at Mukden, during several Japanese attacks. By the war's end, each regiment in the Japanese Army had thee to six machineguns assigned.[166] Mountain guns and hand grenades were also used in almost every attack to give the infantry additional firepower in the front lines.[167] While the Japanese considered indirect artillery fire as a critical multiplier to support infantry, the number of casualties caused by Russian artillery on Japanese troops was relatively low, accounting for less than 10 percent of its total casualties. Machinegun and small arms fires, on the other hand, accounted for 80 to 85 percent of the casualties.[168] The small percentage of total losses caused by Russian artillery fire, can be attributed to the protection offered by hasty fighting positions, as well as Russia's limitations in calling for and adjusting artillery fires during Japanese attacks.

Unique in this battle was the increasing use of modern communications. During the battle, General Nogi's headquarters maintained almost continuous communications with his higher headquarters during a 100-kilometer movement.[169] The Russian commander, at the same time, was plagued by indecision due to poor information and reporting. While General Kuropatkin used modern communications whenever possible, many of his subordinates failed to embrace its use, relying on messengers almost exclusively.[170] The failure of his subordinates to give him accurate timely information was just one of the many reasons for Russia's defeat.

General Kuropatkin also appeared to greatly underestimate the idea of unit cohesion in assigning missions. Throughout the battle, he built composite units to conduct decisive actions, including his 7 March counterattacks. By the time the final retreat was ordered, only two units, the 1st Siberian Corps and the 17th European Corps had not been piecemealed into an attack.[171]

The Japanese victory at Mukden was not the decisive event of the war, but it did contribute significantly to the final Japanese victory. It was only after the destruction of the Japanese Baltic Fleet at Tsushima, and growing unrest in European Russia, that Russia agreed to a peace settlement.

[1]The Russo-Japanese War, Reports from the British Officers Attached to the Japanese Forces in the Field, vol. 2, 297.

[2]General De Negrier, *Lessons of the Russo-Japanese War,* trans. E. Spiers (London: Hugh Rees, Ltd., 1906), 7; Addington, 131; Harries, 90; Weber, 212; and *Reports of Military Observers Attached to the Armies in Manchuria During the Russo-Japanese War,* part 3, 214.

[3]Addington, 131; David Walder, *The Short Victorious War* (New York: Harper and Row, Publishers, 1973, 266-267.

[4]*The Battle of Mukden,* 6; Falls, 165.

[5]Presseisen gives an excellent overview of this transition form all French instructors to a German / French mix. Presseisen, 101-105; English and Gudmundsson, 7; Shumpei Okamoto, *The Japanese Oligarchy and the Russo-Japanese War* (New York: Columbia University Press, 1970), 16-19; and Harries, 48-49.

[6]Okamoto, 19.

[7]Cyril Falls compares Oyama's leadership style to that of Moltke, giving maximum latitude to his subordinate commanders. Japan's Army was influenced not only by its pre-war German advisors, but also by German writers. By 1904, Clausewitz' *On War* was already translated and studied by the Japanese. Falls, 176; Harries, 90; C. Howland, The Russo-Japanese War, Eight lectures by Col. C. R. Howland, 1920-1921, 87, Special Collections, Combined Arms Research Library, USACGSOC, Fort Leavenworth; C. Aspinall, "Interior or Exterior Lines," *The Journal of the Royal United Service Institution* 176 (July 1909), 305; J. Fuller, *The Conduct of War, 1789-1961* (New York: Da Capo Press, 1992), 141; *Reports of Military Observers Attached to the Armies in Manchuria During the Russo-Japanese War,* part 3, 169; Carl von Clausewitz, *On War,* trans. and ed. Michael Howard and Peter Paret (Princeton: Princeton University Press, 1984), 37-38.

[8]Service in the Second Reserve was later extended to 10 years during the war to increase the available manpower pools in Japan. *Reports of the Military Observers to the Armies in Manchuria During the Russo-Japanese War,* part 5, (Washington: Government Printing Office, 1907), 10-12; *Reports of Military Observers Attached to the Armies in Manchuria During the Russo-Japanese War,* part 3, 88-90; Ware, 5; Horsetzky, 6; and Smith, 28.

[9]Some accounts raise the total number of active and trained reserve to 850,000 troops. Anderson, 24; E. Gunter, trans. "The Von Lobell Annual Reports on the Changes and Progress in Military Matters in 1903," *The Journal of the Royal United Service Institution* 320 (October 1904), 1132-1133; Riggs, Lectures: Russo-Japanese War, First Lecture, 8-10; and Horsetzky, 6-7.

[10] By January 1905, Japanese losses were estimated at 120,000. All were replaced prior to the Battle of Mukden. Weber, 180; *The Official German Account of the Russo-Japanese War, Between San-de-pu and Mukden,* trans. Karl Donat (London: Hugh Rees, 1910), 118.

[11] E. Gunter, trans. "The Von Lobell Annual Reports on the Changes and Progress in Military Matters in 1904," *The Journal of the Royal United Service Institution* 336 (February 1906), 227-228. Porter, 315-316; and *Reports of Military Observers Attached to the Armies in Manchuria During the Russo-Japanese War,* part 3, 90-91.

[12] *Reports of the Military Observers to the Armies in Manchuria During the Russo-Japanese War,* part 1, (Washington: Government Printing Office, 1906), 67; *Epitome of the Russo-Japanese War,* 80. "The Von Lobell Annual Reports on the Changes and Progress in Military Matters in 1904," *The Journal of the Royal United Service Institution* 336, 228; and Niessell, "Tactical Lessons Derived from the Russo-Japanese War," 118, 140.

[13] "Précis of Foreign Military Papers, German Papers," *The Journal of the United Service Institution of India* 169 (October 1907), 516; "Japanese Principles of Drill," translated from the *Revised Commentary on the Infantry Drill Regulations of Japan, 8th Edition,* in *Infantry Journal* 1 (July-August 1912), 138.

[14] "The Japanese Infantry Attack," *The Journal of the United States Infantry Association* 3 (January 1905), 16; Janin, 1.

[15] Major Oliver Wood, "Target Practice – Japan," *Journal of the United States Infantry Association* 4 (April 1905), 112-113.

[16] *Official History of the Russo-Japanese War,* part 1, 4.

[17] Pottinger, 78-79; Niessell, *Tactical Lessons Derived from the Russo-Japanese War,* 8; E. Gunter, trans. "The Von Lobell Annual Reports on the Changes and Progress in Military Matters in 1905," *The Journal of the Royal United Service Institution* 345 (November 1906), 1387-1388; *Reports of Military Observers Attached to the Armies in Manchuria During the Russo-Japanese War,* part 3, 14-15; Janin, 3-5, 80.

[18] De Negrier claims that the Japanese abandoned the antiquated methods of the close order attack and adopted new tactics. In fact, the tactic of "extended order" was listed as "main form of fighting for infantry" in the prewar Japanese regulation. The Japanese extended order doctrine is translated in "The Japanese Infantry Attack," 10-12. General De Negier, "Some Lessons of the Russo-Japanese War," translated from *Revue des Deux Monde* in *The Journal of the Royal United Service Institution* 341 (July 1906), 912-913.

[19] The Japanese even dug shallow fighting positions when in the attack. In a two-man team, one soldier would continue to fire while a second soldier would dig out a

position for them both. After this team moved forward, another Japanese element would occupy the positions dug. Japanese companies averaged one entrenching tool per two soldiers (103 tools for 217 soldiers). M. Black, "The Intrenchment (sic) of Infantry During Attack," *Internationale Revue uber die gesamten Armeen und Flotten,* trans. Raymond Sheldon, *Journal of the United States Infantry* 2 (October 1906), 151; "Military Notes," *The Journal of the Royal United Service Institution* 332 (October 1905), 1213; Niessell, *Tactical Lessons Derived from the Russo-Japanese War*, 9; "German Papers," 516; "The Von Lobell Annual Reports on the Changes and Progress in Military Matters in 1905," 1399.

[20]To ease the movement of this cumbersome protection, the bags were often fitted with carrying straps. Luigi Giannitrapani, *The Russo Japanese War,* vol. 2, trans. Frank Harris, Special Collections, Combined Arms Research Library, Fort Leavenworth, Kansas, 1907, 64-66; Black, "The Intrenchment (sic) of Infantry During Attack," 152; Janin, 85; "Precis of Foreign Military Papers," *The Journal of the United Services Institution of India* 174 (January 1909), 138-139.

[21]The Japanese even used sand bags as cover during their attacks into the mountains east of Mukden. *Official History (Naval and Military) of the Russo-Japanese War,* vol. 3, 278.

[22]W. Kirton, "With the Japanese on the Yalu," *The Journal of the Royal United Service Institution* 325 (March 1905), 279; Janin, 85-86; Gustav Wrangel, "The Cavalry in the East Asiatic Campaign," trans. Harry Bell, *Journal of the U.S. Cavalry Association* 67 (January 1908), 496; *The Russo-Japanese War, Reports from the British Officers Attached to the Japanese Forces in the Field,* vol. 2, 676; "Military Notes," *The Journal of the Royal United Service Institution* 336 (February 1906), 248-249; "Precis of Foreign Military Journals," *The Journal of the United Service Institution of India* 165 (October 1906), 455-456.

[23]To support an attack, the Japanese developed the tactic of placing grenadiers 15 meter in front of the first line of advancing troops, to allow them to us grenade for their shock effect as the infantry advanced. "The Von Lobell Annual Reports on the Changes and Progress in Military Matters in 1905," 1399-1400; Giannitrapani, 63-64; Janin, 95; *The Russo-Japanese War, Reports from the British Officers Attached to the Japanese Forces in the Field,* vol. 2, 307-308.

[24]In most accounts, the total forces of the Japanese and Russians are described in number of battalions and regiments. The Japanese Armies in the north are deducted by the fact that at the beginning of the war, Japan had 13 divisions. As the war progressed, each of these armies would receive additional forces in the form of Kobi or reserve brigade's, as discussed in the Port Arthur chapter. Kennedy, 301; Horsetzky, 6-7.

[25]*The Russo-Japanese War, Reports from the British Officers Attached to the Japanese Forces in the Field,* vol. 2, 219; Kuhn, "From Port Arthur to Mukden with Nogi,", 801.

²⁶Kuropatkin was present at the decisive battle of Plevna, serving as the chief of Staff to Major General Skobelev, a famous Russian commander. *Studies in Battle Command,* (Fort Leavenworth: U.S. Government Printing Office, 1998), 79-83; Menning, 93; Kuropatkin, vol. 1, viii.

²⁷Menning, 93; Falls, 176.

²⁸The overall commander of Russia's Far East Forces was Viceroy (Admiral) Eugene Alexieff, whose appointment was solely based on his connections with the Russian Royal family. Kuropatkin was placed in over all control of the Far East in October 1904. Kuropatkin, vol. 1, p. viii; Walder, 55; and Connaughton, 221.

²⁹Falls, 176-177; Menning, 93-94.

³⁰William Maxwell, an observer with the Japanese Army, cited a Japanese copy of a report by Kuropatkin's superior in the Russo-Turkish War. It stated "you are an ambitious man and will have a fine career…(but) never accept an independent post in which you will have to direct affairs." Maxwell, 13-17.

³¹*The Russo-Japanese War; Russian Official Account,* part 1, trans. Claudine Wannamaker, 1937, 37-38, Special Collections, Combined Arms Research Library, USACGSOC, Fort Leavenworth.

³²Reichmann, 28.

³³Prior to his visit to the Far East, Kuropatkin proclaimed Port Arthur could resist a force five times stronger. *The Russo-Japanese War; Russian Official Account,* part 1, 28-29; *The Russo-Japanese War; Russian Official Account,* part 1, 42-60; Birnie, 196-197.

³⁴Major H. Blore, "Northern Army Prize Essay, 1912," *The Journal of the United Service Institution of India* 191 (April 1913), 146.

³⁵General Kuropatkin identified the key to Russia's ability to wage a successful war in the Far East as maintaining access to the 5,000-mile Trans-Siberian Railroad to European Russia. At the beginning of the war this route only supported seven trains a day and it took as long as six weeks to move a Russian corps and its equipment from European Russia to the Far East. The major constraint of the rail line was that it was not complete. To cross Lake Baikal in Siberia, trains had to cross on a specially built ferry that transported 27 cars on three internal tracks. In the winter months, railroad track was laid across the ice to the far side of the lake. It was not until September 1904 that the line around the lake was finally completed. Once completed, the number of trains from European Russia was increased to 17-18 per day. The dependence on this single supply route significantly restricted Russia's movements during the war and the fear of losing access to this critical line of communication impacted every attempt by Russia to gain the initiative. Lieutenant Colonel Yoda, "Modern Tendencies in Strategy and Tactics as Shown in Campaign in the Far East," *Kaikosha Kiji* 352 (December 1906), trans. E.

Calthrop in *The Journal of the Royal United Service Institution* 353 (July 1907), 855; E. Gunter, trans. "The Von Lobell Annual Reports on the Changes and Progress in Military Matters in 1904," *The Journal of the Royal United Service Institution* 334 (December 1905), 1410-1411; Cloman, 55, 61; Porter 170-171; Aspinall, 306; Sedgwick, *The Russo-Japanese War, A Sketch*, 73; *The Russo-Japanese War; Russian Official Account,* Part I, 42; Kuropatkin, vol. 1, 261; "The Von Lobell Annual Reports on the Changes and Progress in Military Matters in 1904," *The Journal of the Royal United Service Institution* 336, 226; Alexei Kuropatkin, *The Russian Army and the Japanese War,* vol. 2. trans. A. Lindsay, ed. E. Swinton (New York: E. P. Dutton, 1909), 196; John Barnes, "Theater of War," *Journal of the United States Infantry Association* 4 (January 1908), 594; Early Duncan, "Plans and Operations of the Japanese Fourth Army, 1 July – 27 August 1904," 1931, 3, Special Collections, Combined Arms Research Library, Fort Leavenworth, Kansas, Group Report; Maguire, 4.

[36]*Reports of Military Observers Attached to the Armies in Manchuria During the Russo-Japanese War,* part 3, 159; Maguire, 3-4; and Footslogger, 26.

[37]Porter, 169; Kuropatkin, vol. 1, 271.

[38]Kuropatkin, vol. 1, 270.

[39]This number included 98,000 maneuver troops, 25,000 fortress troops (spread between Port Arthur and Vladivostok), and 24,000-30,000 soldiers assigned as security detachments along the rail network. Macomb, 1015; Menning, 153-54; and Hargreaves, 20.

[40]Horsetsky, 5.

[41]Niessell, Tactical Lessons Derived from the Russo-Japanese War," 117; Kuropatkin, vol. 1, 282.

[42]Reichmann, 10.

[43]These Second Class Reserves averaged 35 years of age, much older than the average recruit. Major M. Macomb, "The Russian Infantry Soldier," *The Journal of the Royal United Service Institution* 342 (August 1906), 1014; and Horestzky, 4.

[44]Kuropatkin, vol. 1, 275.

[45]*Reports of Military Observers attached to the Armies in Manchuria During the Russo-Japanese War*, part 5 (Washington: Government Printing Office, 1907), 176.

[46]Ibid., 271-273; Ware, 5.

[47]"After Mukden: A Russian Verdict on Russian Failures," *Russian Gazette*, trans by W. Bingham in *The Journal of the Royal United Service Institution* 328 (June 1905), 686; Kuropatkin, vol. 1, 274-275, 278.

[48]Kuropatkin, vol. 1, 274-276; Macomb, "The Russian Infantry Soldier," 1015.

[49]How much marksmanship training newly soldiers received prior to moving to Manchuria could not be determined by available documents. Captain S. Slocum, "Target Practice – Russia," *Journal of the United States Infantry Association* 4 (April 1905), 106-107.

[50]Of the 20 round allocated to familiarize newly mobilized forces, five were committed to volley fire training. Ibid.

[51]Fuller, *A History of the Western World*, vol. 3, 166.

[52]"Infantry Combat in the Russo-Japanese War," translated from *Revue Militaire des Armees Etrangeres* in *The Journal of the Royal United Service Institution* 342 (August 1906), 1050; Falls, 177.

[53]L. Soloviev, *Actual Experiences in War: Battle Action of the Infantry; Impressions of a Company Commander* (Washington: War Department, 1906), 27; Maguire, 4.

[54]Kuropatkin, vol. 1, 274, 278; Maguire, 4.

[55]L. Soloviev, 18; "After Mukden: A Russian Verdict on Russian Failures," 692.

[56]Niessell, Tactical Lessons Derived from the Russo-Japanese War, 119-121.

[57]"Military Notes," No. 333, 1330.

[58]See the following references for abbreviated accounts of these battles. W. Bird, "The Battle of Te-Li-Szu," *The Journal of the United Service Institution of India* 191 (April 1913); Adolf Horsetzky, *An Epitome of the Russo-Japanese War of 1904-1905*, trans. Harry Bell. (Vienna: Seidel and Son, 1915; Fort Leavenworth: Army Services School, 1916); C. Howland, The Russo-Japanese War, Eight lectures by Col. C. R. Howland, 1920-1921, Special Collections, Combined Arms Research Library, USACGSOC, Fort Leavenworth; and *Lectures on the Russo-Japanese War, Officers of the Japanese General Staff*. Translated by the American Embassy, Tokyo, 1906, Special Collections, Combined Arms Research Library, Fort Leavenworth, Kansas.

[59]K. Riggs, Lectures: Russo-Japanese War, Eighth Lecture, n.d., 1; Special Collections, Combined Arms Research Library, USACGSOC, Fort Leavenworth; and Horsetzky, 64.

[60]The Japanese would have to wait another two full months for the Port Arthur's fall. Leslie Saul, "Why did Russia Lose in Her War with Japan?" Individual Report, 1930, 6, Special Collections, Combined Arms Research Library, USACGSOC, Fort Leavenworth.

[61] "Asiaticus" (pseudonym), *Reconnaissance in the Russo-Japanese War,* trans. J. Montgomery (London: Hugh Rees, Ltd., 1908), 114-115.

[62] The actual committed force for this raid varies by account, ranging from 5,000 to as many as 10,000. To support this attack, the Russians employed 1,500 pack animals to carry supplies. Serge Nidoine, "The Russian Cavalry During the Russo-Japanese War," *Journal des Science Militaires* (August 1905). Translated by Herschel Tupes in *Journal of the United States Cavalry* 64 (April 1907), 739; K. Lancers, "A Precis of a Study of the Russo-Japanese War by "Chasseur,"" *The Journal of the United Services Institution of India* 163 (April 1906), 154; De Negrier, *Lessons of the Russo-Japanese War* 23.

[63] Russia lost 340 soldiers during the raid. "Asiaticus," 117-119; Nidoine, 691, 739-740; and "What Lessons Can the Cavalry Draw from the Russo-Japanese War?" *Militar-Wochenblatt* (December 1906), translated by Walter Kruger for *Journal of the U.S. Cavalry Association* 65 (July 1907), 130-131, and Horsetzky, 69.

[64] Prior to the arrival of the Third Japanese Army in the north, Russia forces outnumbered those of Japan by approximately 80,000 men. *The Official German Account of the Russo-Japanese War, Yin-Kou and San-de-pu,* trans. Karl Donat (London: Hugh Rees, 1910), 6, 54-55, 116-117, 137-141.

[65] Ibid., 137-141.

[66] Russia committed only 86,800 of an available 320,000 against and initial 70,000 Japanese defenders at San-De-Pu. The Russian ground commander, Lieutenant General Grippenberg had requested additional forces to be committed, but was denied by General Kuropatkin. Kuropatkin maintained the large reserve during the battle, fearing a Japanese counterattack in the east, against his center. Weber, 184-189; *The Official German Account of the Russo-Japanese War, Yin-Kou and San-de-pu,* 6, 122; and Horsetzky, 70.

[67] *Epitome of the Russo-Japanese War,* 100-101.

[68] Ibid., 101; Weber, 184; and Riggs, Lectures: Russo-Japanese War, Eighth Lecture, 6.

[69] *The Official German Account of the Russo-Japanese War, Yin-Kou and San-de-pu,* 114; Weber 188.

[70] Howland, 77; Weber, 190.

[71] Captain Aubert, "Russian Cavalry at Mukden," *Kavalleristische Monatshefte,* translated by Harry Bell in *Journal of the U.S. Cavalry Association* 68 (April 1908), 746; Lancers, 155-156.

[72] Lancers, 156.

[73] After this raid, false reports reached General Kuropatkin that the Japanese had a force of 10,000 troops staged in Mongolia to interdict his lines of communications, further raising his fear of interdiction attacks to his rear. Kuropatkin, vol. 2, 268; Ware, 7; Porter, 204; Lancers, 156; Horsetzky, 73; Howland, 67-69; and Aubert, 746.

[74] *Reports of Military Observers Attached to the Armies in Manchuria During the Russo-Japanese War,* part 1, 229-230; Archdale, 285.

[75] *The Russo-Japanese War, Reports from the British Officers Attached to the Japanese Forces in the Field,* vol. 2, 219.

[76] N. Taylor, "The Battle of Mukden," *The Journal of the United Service Institution of India* 176 (July 1909), 349; *The Battle of Mukden,* 12.

[77] Kobi or reserve units were raised in Japan to supplement the Japanese main divisions. Several Kobi brigades were raised during the war.

[78] The Kobi or reserve division was formed in late October, so it had a developed staff by the time of the advance in February. *The Official German Account of the Russo-Japanese War, Between San-de-pu and Mukden,* 114-116.

[79] *The Russo-Japanese War, Reports from the British Officers Attached to the Japanese Forces in the Field,* vol. 2, 86.

[80] *The Official German Account of the Russo-Japanese War, Between San-de-pu and Mukden,* 120-122; Howland, 80.

[81] *The Official German Account of the Russo-Japanese War, Between San-de-pu and Mukden,* 119, 145; Howland, 80; *The Russo-Japanese War, Reports from the British Officers Attached to the Japanese Forces in the Field,* vol. 2, 297.

[82] *Epitome of the Russo-Japanese War,* 105-108.

[83] *Official History (Naval and Military) of the Russo-Japanese War,* vol. 3, 268.

[84] De Negrier states this screening force consisted of 6,500 cavalry and 1,000 foot soldiers, with supporting artillery. De Negrier, *Lessons of the Russo-Japanese War,* 34; David Fraser, "The Cavalry Lessons of the War," *Journal of U.S. Cavalry Association* 59 (January 1906), 489; *The Russo-Japanese War, Reports from the British Officers Attached to the Japanese Forces in the Field,* vol. 2, 231-233; and Weber, 200.

[85] K., C., "Japanese Ruses of War," *Militar-Wochenblatt* 78 (June 1905), translated in *The Journal of the Royal United Service Institution* 332 (October 1905), 1188-1190.

[86] *Epitome of the Russo-Japanese War,* 105-108.

[87]Riggs, Lectures: Russo-Japanese War, Eighth Lecture, 10-11; Holand, 81; *The Official German Account of the Russo-Japanese War, Between San-de-pu and Mukden*, 121, 144-149; *The Battle of Mukden*, 20-23; *Epitome of the Russo-Japanese War*, 105-108.

[88]Accounts vary as to the actual strength of the Japanese forces at Mukden. Some accounts claim as few as 200,000 men to as many as 400,000. Some of this confusion appears to be based on whether support troops and organic cavalry are counted in the total troop counts. The numbers listed are in general, the most common numbers recorded. The number of machineguns is given as 200 in all accounts except the British Official History. *Official History (Naval and Military) of the Russo-Japanese War*, Vol. III, 268-269; *Epitome of the Russo-Japanese War*, 108; *The Official German Account of the Russo-Japanese War, Between San-de-pu and Mukden*, 118; Lancers, 156; *The Battle of Mukden*, 10; "Military Notes," 1332.

[89]Vincent, 34.

[90]Lieutenant Colonel Frocard and Captain Painvin, "Communications on the Battle-field," *La Revue D' Infantrerie,* translated in *The Journal of the Royal United Service Institution* 373 (March 1909), 369; *The Russo-Japanese War, Reports from the British Officers Attached to the Japanese Forces in the Field,* vol. 2, 214.

[91]Joseph Kuhn, "Report on the Operations of the Japanese Armies during the Russo-Japanese War" n.d., 43, Special Collections, Combined Arms Research Library, Fort Leavenworth, Kansas; Niessel, "Tactical Lessons Derived from the Russo-Japanese War," 129.

[92]"Military Notes," 129.

[93]Vincent, 33-34.

[94]Both the Third Army in the west and the Fifth Japanese Army in the mountainous terrain in the east were able to maintain telegraph communications with Marshal Oyama throughout the battle. Yoda, 857; Frocard and Painvin, 369; *Reports of Military Observers Attached to the Armies in Manchuria During the Russo-Japanese War,* part 3, 231; Taylor, 157; and *The Russo-Japanese War, Reports from the British Officers Attached to the Japanese Forces in the Field,* vol. 2, 228.

[95]General De Negrier, "Some Lessons of the Russo-Japanese War," *Revue Des Deux Mondes,* Translated in *The Journal of the Royal United Service Institution* 339 (May 1906), 694.

[96]Total strength numbers vary just as the Japanese numbers vary, with the lowest reported at 275,000 and the highest reported at 375,000. Most accounts agree on the number of artillery pieces present at the battle, however, the number of committed machineguns varies between fifty-four and eighty-eight, with eighty-eight being the most often reported number. Montgomery Macomb, "Machine Guns in the Russian Army,"

Journal of the United States Infantry Association 3 (January 1907), 16; William Johnson, "The Infantry Machine-gun Detachment," *Journal of the United States Infantry Association* 3 (November 1907), 393; *Official German Account of the Russo-Japanese War, Between San-de-pu and Mukden*, 118; *The Battle of Mukden*, 9; Taylor, 349; *Epitome of the Russo-Japanese War*, 105; Menning, 186-87; Fuller, *A Military History of the Western World*, vol. 3, 165.

[97]Taylor, 349; Riggs, Lectures: Russo-Japanese War, Eighth Lecture, 8; Horsetzky, 75; and De Negrier, "Some Lessons of the Russo-Japanese War," 694.

[98]Riggs, Lectures: Russo-Japanese War, Eighth Lecture, 8; Niessel, *Lessons Derived from the Russo-Japanese War*, 129.

[99]*The Battle of Mukden*, 11; Taylor, 349.

[100]The commander on the ground at San-De-Pu, Lieutenant General Grippenberg, was removed and left for St. Petersburg three days after the battle. *Epitome of the Russo-Japanese War*, 101; *The Battle of Mukden*, 13.

[101]Kuropatkin, vol. 2, 271.

[102]*Epitome of the Russo-Japanese War*, 105; Taylor, 350; *The Battle of Mukden*, 14.

[103]Giannitrapani, *The Russo Japanese War*, vol. 2, 58; Weber, 201-202.

[104]Translated letters taken from dead Japanese soldiers also reinforced the belief that portions or all of the Third Japanese Army was in the east. "Japanese Ruses of War," 1189-1190.

[105]Japanese press accounts had openly noted that the Japanese Fifth Army was moving on the east of the rest of the Japanese force. It also stated that the Fifth Army had 8 divisions and 140,000 troops. How much of this information actually reached General Kuropatkin is not known. "The Von Lobell Annual Reports on the Changes and Progress in Military Matters in 1904," *The Journal of the Royal United Service Institution* 336, 227; De Negier, "Some Lessons of the Russo-Japanese War," 695; Kuropatkin, vol. 2, 271.

[106]On 25 February, as the situation developed in the east, General Kuropatkin's intelligence officer informed him that he has indications that the Third Japanese Army was not in the east, but in the west. Kuropatkin did not accept the significance of this information as at the same time, he also received a false report that the Japanese were moving additional forces toward the east. Horsetsky, 77-78; Howland, 81; *The Battle of Mukden*, 14; Riggs, Lectures: Russo-Japanese War, Eighth Lecture, 9; *The Official German Account of the Russo-Japanese War, Yin-Kou and San-de-pu*, 164-168; and De Negrier, "Some Lessons of the Russo-Japanese War," 695.

[107] By February 25, the Russians began moving 200 battalions to defend against the attacks of 70 Japanese battalions in the mountains in the east. Horsetzky, 78; Giannitrapani, *The Russo Japanese War,* vol. 2, 58-59; Riggs, Lectures: Russo-Japanese War, First Lecture, 11; and Weber, 202.

[108] *Epitome of the Russo-Japanese War,* 112-114; *The Russo-Japanese War, Reports from the British Officers Attached to the Japanese Forces in the Field,* vol. 2, 242-245; Taylor, 157; and Riggs, Lectures: Russo-Japanese War, Eighth Lecture, 10.

[109] As covered earlier, the mission of the Japanese Fourth Army's during this phase of the Battle of Mukden was primarily to hold the Russian troops to its front in place. On the day of the attack, the Japanese were still in their initial prepared positions. *The Battle of Mukden,* 18; *The Official German Account of the Russo-Japanese War, Battle of Mukden,* part 1, 54-56.

[110] The 11-inch guns deployed north from Port Arthur supported the Second and Fourth Army's artillery. Riggs, Lectures: Russo-Japanese War, Eighth Lecture, 10-11; Weber, 205; "Military Notes," 1332; and "The Von Lobell Annual Reports on the Changes and Progress in Military Matters in 1905," 1399.

[111] The cavalry of the Second Army initially covered the gap between the Second and Third Army. As the gap expanded, the Army began to advance its ground forces to close the gap. *The Russo-Japanese War, Reports from the British Officers Attached to the Japanese Forces in the Field,* vol. 2, 95; *The Official German Account of the Russo-Japanese War, Battle of Mukden,* part 1. trans. Karl Donat (London: Hugh Rees, 1914), 118.

[112] *Reports of Military Observers attached to the Armies in Manchuria During the Russo-Japanese War*, part 4 (Washington: Government Printing Office, 1907), 431-435.

[113] The Russian cavalry maintained almost constant contact with the Japanese move. On the 28th, the Russian Cavalry reported that "more than a division" was advancing. This report was forwarded to General Kuropatkin's headquarters. Aubert, 746-747; "What Lessons can the Cavalry Draw from the Russo-Japanese War," 132; Taylor, 351; Nidoine, 687; *The Official German Account of the Russo-Japanese War, Battle of Mukden,* part 1, 71; Horsetzky, 789.

[114] Weber, 205; Ira Swift, "Historical Analysis of Envelopment in the Battles of; The Franco-Prussian War, The Russo-Japanese War, The World War," Individual Report, 1935, 27, Special Collections, Combined Arms Research Library, Fort Leavenworth, Kansas.

[115] Kuropatkin, vol. 2, 274-275; Horsetzky, 80; Swift, 27.

[116] *The Battle of Mukden,* 25; Howland, 83; *Epitome of the Russo-Japanese War,* 116.

[117] *The Battle of Mukden,* 18-19; Kuropatkin, vol. 2, 276.

[118] Howland, 81; Kuropatkin, vol. 2, 275; *Epitome of the Russo-Japanese War,* 118; Giannitrapani, *The Russo-Japanese War*, vol. 2, 71.

[119] Taylor, 352.

[120] The two brigades were formed into a cavalry division and given two additional batteries of artillery and six machineguns. Howland, 82; Giannitrapani, *The Russo-Japanese War*, vol. 2, 74; *Reports of Military Observers attached to the Armies in Manchuria During the Russo-Japanese War*, part 3, 208; *The Official German Account of the Russo-Japanese War, Battle of Mukden,* part 1., 149, 160; De Negrier, *Lessons of the Russo-Japanese War,* 35.

[121] *Reports of Military Observers attached to the Armies in Manchuria During the Russo-Japanese War*, part 3, 208.

[122] *Reports of Military Observers attached to the Armies in Manchuria During the Russo-Japanese War*, part 4, 443; Horsetzky, 83.

[123] *Epitome of the Russo-Japanese War,* 127; *Reports of Military Observers attached to the Armies in Manchuria During the Russo-Japanese War*, part 3, 210.

[124] *Official History (Naval and Military) of the Russo-Japanese War,* vol. 3, 376-378.

[125] *Epitome of the Russo-Japanese War,* 128-129.

[126] The defending Russians in front of the Fourth Japanese Army belonged to the 1st European Corps, one of the few non-Asiatic Russian corps then committed at Mukden. [126] Giannitrapani, *The Russo-Japanese War*, vol. 2, 64-65.

[127] *The Russo-Japanese War, Reports from the British Officers Attached to the Japanese Forces in the Field,* vol. 2, 245-246.

[128] Giannitrapani, *The Russo-Japanese War*, vol. 2, 64-66

[129] To ease the movement of this cumbersome protection, the bags were often fitted with carrying straps. Giannitrapani, *The Russo-Japanese War*, vol. 2, 64-66; Black, "The Intrenchment (sic) of Infantry During Attack," 152; and Janin, 85.

[130] Howland, 85; Giannitrapani, *The Russo-Japanese War*, Vol. II, 67; "The Von Lobell Annual Reports on the Changes and Progress in Military Matters in 1905," 1399.

[131] M. Kinai, *The Russo-Japanese War (Official Reports),* vol. 2 (London: Kegan Paul, Trench, Taubner & Co., Ltd., n.d.), 82.

¹³²*The Russo-Japanese War, Reports from the British Officers Attached to the Japanese Forces in the Field,* vol. 2, 247; *The Battle of Mukden,* 20; *The Official German Account of the Russo-Japanese War, Battle of Mukden,* part 1, 140-141.

¹³³*The Russo-Japanese War, Reports from the British Officers Attached to the Japanese Forces in the Field,* vol. 2, 245-247; Howland, 84; *The Official German Account of the Russo-Japanese War, Battle of Mukden,* part 1, 183-184.

¹³⁴Taylor, 354; Kinai, *The Russo-Japanese War (Official Reports),* vol. 2, 82.

¹³⁵In some cases the artillery batteries were moved a gun at a time to ensure fires were maintained for units in contact. Ibid., 439-440; Janin, 77; *Reports of Military Observers attached to the Armies in Manchuria During the Russo-Japanese War,* part 3, 270, 273-274.

¹³⁶*The Russo-Japanese War, Reports from the British Officers Attached to the Japanese Forces in the Field,* vol. 2, 108.

¹³⁷Giannitrapani, *The Russo-Japanese War,* vol. 2, 62; *The Russo-Japanese War, Reports from the British Officers Attached to the Japanese Forces in the Field,* vol. 2, 119; E. Wood (Major), "Gold Medal Prize Essay, 1907" *The Journal of the United Service Institution of India* 169 (October 1907), 422-423.

¹³⁸General Kuropatkin ordered the Second Army Commander, Lieutenant General Kaulbars to coordinate the counterattack on the village. *Official History (Naval and Military) of the Russo-Japanese War,* vol. 3, 552.

¹³⁹At this point in the war, the Russian infantry were equipped with a stick grenade that ignited on impact by a fulminating cap in the head of the grenade. Giannitrapani, *The Russo-Japanese War,* vol. 2, 72.

¹⁴⁰One author estimated the losses to the Russians at between 6 and 10,000. *The Russo-Japanese War, Reports from the British Officers Attached to the Japanese Forces in the Field,* vol. 2, 120-122; Giannitrapani, *The Russo-Japanese War,* vol. 2, 80-82; *Reports of Military Observers attached to the Armies in Manchuria During the Russo-Japanese War,* part 4, 454-455; *Official History (Naval and Military) of the Russo-Japanese War,* vol. 3, 550-556.

¹⁴¹The two divisions were the 25th and a composite division made up from several battalions of the 10th Russian Corps. *The Battle of Mukden,* 19; *Reports of Military Observers attached to the Armies in Manchuria During the Russo-Japanese War,* part 3, 207.

¹⁴²*The Battle of Mukden,* 23-24; Howland, 83.

¹⁴³*The Battle of Mukden,* 24; Riggs, Lectures: Russo-Japanese War, Eighth Lecture, 14.

¹⁴⁴Howland, 84.

¹⁴⁵General Kuropatkin initially desired the attack to begin on 4 March, but the troops were not in a position to attack at that time. In the end, the attack was pushed back two days. Kuropatkin also failed to give exacting guidance to General Kaulbars in the extent and desired end state of the attack. *The Official German Account of the Russo-Japanese War, Battle of Mukden,* part 1, 193-200.

¹⁴⁶The use of makeshift units to conduct missions, especially counterattacks, was common practice throughout the war, but proved to greatly degrade any since of cohesion that the counterattacking unit might possess. This practice was also executed in the 1877-1878 Russo-Turkish War. "The Von Lobell Annual Reports on the Changes and Progress in Military Matters in 1904," *The Journal of the Royal United Service Institution* 333, 1278; Giannitrapani, *The Russo-Japanese War*, vol. 2, 44.

¹⁴⁷Lieutenant General Kaulbars, commander of the Russian Second Army, only committed two of his available divisions to the planned counterattack. There were a total of 110 infantry battalions available for the counter attack. Kaulbars planned to only use 33 battalions for the attack. After the war, Gerneral Kuropatkin, who was relieved after the loss at Mukden, was highly critical of Kaulbars for his failure to commit all of his available forces in the counter attack. *The Battle of Mukden,* 28-29; Kuropatkin, vol. 2, 278-279; Giannitrapani, *The Russo-Japanese War*, vol. 2, 76; Weber, 208; Horsetzky, 84-85; and Kuropatkin, vol. 2, 291-296.

¹⁴⁸*The Battle of Mukden,* 32-33; Horsetzky, 86; and Giannitrapani, *The Russo-Japanese War*, vol. 2, 78.

¹⁴⁹The attack was carried out by a small cavalry patrol of Third Army's new cavalry division, and not by the entire force. Lancers, 158; Aubert, 752-753; *The Battle of Mukden*, 37; Weber, 214; and *The Russo-Japanese War, Reports from the British Officers Attached to the Japanese Forces in the Field,* vol. 2, 233.

¹⁵⁰*Official History (Naval and Military) of the Russo-Japanese War,* vol. 3, 559.

¹⁵¹*Epitome of the Russo-Japanese War,* 129; Kinai, *The Russo-Japanese War (Official Reports),* vol. 2, 108; Giannitrapani, *The Russo-Japanese War*, vol. 2, 91; *The Battle of Mukden,* 21.

¹⁵²*The Battle of Mukden,* 41; Howland, 85-86; and Giannitrapani, *The Russo-Japanese War*, vol. 2, 89.

¹⁵³Weber, 211; Horsetzky, 88.

¹⁵⁴Weber, 211, 214; Riggs, Lectures: Russo-Japanese War, Eighth Lecture, 16.

[155] *Official History (Naval and Military) of the Russo-Japanese War,* vol. 3, 631-632; Kuropatkin, vol. 2, 283.

[156] Forty-eight battalions were assigned the task of covering the withdrawal. Giannitrapani, *The Russo-Japanese War*, vol. 2, 86. Riggs in his account states that only 28 battalions were assembled. His number seems low, as the total Russian force numbered over 370 battalions. Riggs, Lectures: Russo-Japanese War, Eighth Lecture, 16.

[157] *The Russo-Japanese War, Reports from the British Officers Attached to the Japanese Forces in the Field,* vol. 2, 227-228, 251; Kuhn, "From Port Arthur to Mukden with Nogi," 802.

[158] *Epitome of the Russo-Japanese War,* 134; Horsetzky, 61; and *Official History (Naval and Military) of the Russo-Japanese War,* vol. 3, 722.

[159] Horsetzky, 91; Giannitrapani, *The Russo-Japanese War*, vol. 2, 84.

[160] Even though only two Japanese divisions committed to the pursuit, General Kuropatkin ordered the retreat further north after he perceived a stronger threat to his force. *The Russo-Japanese War, Reports from the British Officers Attached to the Japanese Forces in the Field,* vol. 2, 286-294, 325-338; *The Battle of Mukden,* 54.

[161] The Japanese Official Report gives the total Russian losses as exceeding 110,000, with a prisoner count of 40,000 and the killed in action number at 26,500. Most observer accounts report the Russian losses at 96,500, including 2,457 officers (10 of these were general officers). Kinai, *The Russo-Japanese War (Official Reports),* vol. 2, 115; *The Battle of Mukden,* 51, 54; Horsetzky, 91; Giannitrapani, *The Russo-Japanese War*, vol. 2, 93; *Epitome of the Russo-Japanese War,* 134; and Taylor, 355.

[162] *The Battle of Mukden,* 35; Horsetzky, 85; Howland, 85.

[163] Kinai, *The Russo-Japanese War (Official Reports),* vol. 2, 115;

[164] *The Russo-Japanese War, Reports from the British Officers Attached to the Japanese Forces in the Field,* vol. 2, 252.

[165] Ibid.

[166] *The Russo-Japanese War, Reports from the British Officers Attached to the Japanese Forces in the Field,* vol. 2, 346; Niessel, "Tactical Lessons derived from the Russo-Japanese War," 102; Henry Reilly, "Machine Gun Organization," *Journal of the United States Cavalry Association* 72 (April 1909), 802.

[167] *The Russo-Japanese War, Reports from the British Officers Attached to the Japanese Forces in the Field,* vol. 2, 273-274, 307..

[168] Niessel, "Tactical Lessons derived from the Russo-Japanese War," 124; *The Russo-Japanese War, Reports from the British Officers Attached to the Japanese Forces in the Field,* vol. 2, 179; *The Russo-Japanese War, Reports from the British Officers Attached to the Japanese Forces in the Field,* vol. 2, 154.

[169] Horsetzky, 91; Giannitrapani, *The Russo-Japanese War,* vol. 2, 96.

[170] Douglas Story, *The Campaign with Kuropatkin,* London: T. Werner Laurie, 1905), 253.

[171] Giannitrapani, *The Russo-Japanese War,* vol. 2, 90.

CHAPTER 4

CONCLUSION

> Machineguns must be brought up and entrenched . . . artillery fire must accompany the infantry to the very last stage of the attack . . .storming infantry must throw hand grenades inside the hostile positions; the final bayonet charge must be delivered when close to the position; while the heavy howitzer shells continue to burst in and behind the position.[1]
>
> General Friederich von Bernhardi, *On War Today*

The observer and professional journal accounts of the Russo-Japanese War clearly illustrate the effects of weapons that would later prove devastating on the World War I battlefield. As seen in the above narrative histories of Port Arthur and Mukden, the observer nations who later fought World War I had adequate examples of the future battlefield as they prepared for the next war. Why these same nations failed to consider these lessons for the next war, is beyond the scope of this paper.

Reports from the Siege of Port Arthur and the Battle for Mukden demonstrated the lethality of 20th Century weapons on a fixed and maneuver battlefield. As the Russo-Japanese War was the first conflict between two European-type armies in thirty years, the war drew military and civilian observers from almost every major western power.[2] These observers wrote exhaustive accounts that provide both wide and narrow viewpoints of the war that provided excellent events learning tools.

Observers were present in both the Japanese and Russian camps during the war. The majority of the accounts published, however, were taken from the Japanese point of view. Many of the observers who were with the Russian Armies in the north left Manchuria in the autumn of 1904, after determining that their Russian hosts provided little to enhance their professional learning. These observers, representing members of the British, French, Austrian, and Swiss governments, departed prior to experiencing the discomforts of the Manchurian winter of 1904-1905.[3] The British, who wrote three different multi-volume official accounts of the war, wrote only one volume dedicated to observers of the Russian forces. This volume, although extremely detailed, ends its account in September 1904 after the Battle of Liao-Yang.[4]

One of the most comprehensive and arguably most balanced accounts of the Russian side of the war was written and published by the Russian General Staff Academy. Printed between 1910 and 1913, this five part, nine-volume work was translated by both the German and French General Staffs for their use.[5] This account, critiques both Russian and Japanese decisions during the war.

The final British account, *Official History of the Russo-Japanese War (Naval and Military)*, was published in three large text volumes and two containers of maps. This history provides a balanced account of the war that identifies many lessons for study. Unfortunately, like the Russian General Staff account, it was completed too late for use as a guide for preparations for World War I and was soon overshadowed by that war.[6]

In addition to the Russian and British reports, the General Staffs of Germany, Austria-Hungary, and the United States also wrote multi-volume accounts of the war. The Austria-Hungary account consisted of eight volumes and the German account consisted of seven volumes. The United States' account was written in four parts, with eight total volumes. The United States' final volume about the war, *Epitome of the Russo-Japanese War*, provides an excellent condensed overview of the war that is only equaled by an Austrian account of the same name.[7] Unlike the later British and Russian reports of the war, the observer accounts from Germany, and the United States, were written and published soon after the end of the war and provided excellent details of the conflict. Likewise, many professional journal accounts about the Russo-Japanese War were written soon after the war's conclusion.

As discussed in the introductory chapter, many of the observers of the Russo-Japanese War would later rise to command units at the general officer level in the First World War. In addition to Lieutenant General Sir Ian Hamilton, who commanded the allied forces at Gallipoli, the World War I British Chief of the Imperial General Staff, Sir William Nicholson was also present in Manchuria as an observer. Along with Captain Max Hoffmann, the future architect of the German Tannenberg victory, Major von Etzel, a future German corps commander at Verdun, also served as an observer. Among the French observers was Lieutenant Colonel Corvisart, another officer who would command a corps at Verdun. Major Enrico Caviglia, an Italian observer, served as a corps commander in the First World War, and in 1943, played an influential part in the overthrow of Benito Mussolini.[8] The American observers included eight future general officers. Their number included not only Captain John Pershing and Captain Peyton March, but also a World War I division commander (Major Joseph Kuhn) and Captain William Judson, who headed the American Military Mission to Russia in 1917-1918.[9]

Following the Russo-Japanese War, the militaries of the observer nations debated the true lessons of the war. The Japanese victories at Port Arthur and Mukden, against prepared Russian defenses, led many nations to believe that an army with an unshakable discipline and spirit of patriotic self-sacrifice would overcome the capabilities of all modern weapons. Other nations mistook the Japanese victory as a confirmation of the effectiveness of offensive tactics on the modern battlefield.[10] Some countries chose to ignore the recommendations of its observers and simply rejected them as not suitable their army.[11] The United States, in particular, believed the lessons from the war were unimportant due to the lack of a credible threat.[12] In their final analysis of the war, most nations agreed that infantry attacks against prepared defenses could succeed when conducted by disciplined troops who possessed high moral qualities and a strong national and offensive sprit.[13]

Several countries did make doctrinal changes in their infantry doctrine after the Russo-Japanese War. The British Army published an updated regulation in 1909 that appeared to capture many of the infantry lessons learned in the war. In this regulation, the use of rushes, combined with fire and maneuver, was established as a primary maneuver tactic.[14] An updated German infantry drill regulation, published in May 1906, also updated its infantry tactics. *Drill Regulation of 1906* stated that German formations were to advance in closed formations to within 1,000 meters of their enemy. At that time, artillery fires would be used to force enemy machinegun crews and riflemen to seek cover. If this fire was successful, the German regulation called for a continued advance in tight formations. If the artillery preparatory fires were unsuccessful, German infantry would disperse into platoons and if necessary squads, to conduct rushes forward using available cover. The drill manual did caveat this guidance, however, with the statement that the breaking up of larger formations should be avoided whenever possible.[15] The United States also included extended order fighting as a priority in training. In several pre-World War I articles in the *United States Infantry Association Journal,* extended-order drill and marksmanship training was stressed as critical to infantry success in the future.[16]

The Army of Austria-Hungary chose to ignore the lessons of the dispersed formations and continued training infantry in dense formations for several years after the war.[17] French theorist prior to World War I also discounted the impact of the Russo-Japanese War. Marshal Ferdinand Foch, then commandant of the French War Academy, wrote in 1909 that combat experiences of the Russo-Japanese War were "neither complete nor of immediate interests." He also stated nothing from the war would "affect the fundamental principles of the conduct of war."[18] General De Negrier, another well-written French theorist, also discounted the lessons of the war, stating that quality of the French soldier would overcome any technological advances on the field of battle.[19] One aspect that was ignored by almost every country prior to World War I was the development and integration of new short-range weapons systems.

Many observer countries failed to develop any of the infantry support weapons that proved decisive in the Russo-Japanese War. The development of hand grenades and trench mortars, both crucial to the success of the Japanese at Port Arthur and the close fights at Mukden almost ceased prior to World War I.[20] One British observer considered the effectiveness of the hand grenade as "exaggerated" during the war and wrote in his post-war report that "it (is) doubtful whether sufficient occasion will arise to justify any extended training" in the use of grenades in the future.[21] While both Britain and France did introduce new types of grenades into their inventories after the Russo-Japanese War, production was very limited.[22] The British Expeditionary Force (BEF) of 1914, considered one of the best trained, organized, and equipped forces in Britain's history to that time, deployed with neither hand grenades nor trench mortars.[23] Soon after its arrival in France, the Royal Engineers of the BEF were directed to begin production of ad hoc grenades. Makeshift wood mortars, similar to those developed in the fighting at Port Arthur, were also constructed by the BEF.[24]

The development of a trench mortar to support infantry attacks received no attention after the Russo-Japanese War. Its extensive use during the war was noted in several many accounts, but like the grenade, it usefulness was underestimated until after the beginning of World War I. This underestimation can be partially attributed to several post-war journal accounts that were critical of the accuracy and power of the mortar in relation to artillery.[25] The United States, like the nations of Europe in 1914, did not develop a trench mortar until after it entered World War I. By 1917, France and Britain were using seven different types of trench mortars on the battlefields of Europe.[26]

German development of hand grenades and trench mortars was little better than that of the allied nations. Within two months of declaring war, however, German infantry units, like those of the Allies, quickly identified the utility of the hand grenades in conducting trench warfare. By the end of 1915, Germany began the development of special attack battalions that included a six-man hand grenade team for every platoon.[27] German trench mortar companies were formed as part of German pioneer battalion's early in the war. By 1918, every German infantry battalion had one mortar section assigned and every regiment had a mortar detachment with twelve light and twenty-four medium mortars assigned.[28] While development of grenades and mortars was almost non-existent after the Russo-Japanese War, artillery development continued.

The lessons learned for the use of artillery varied by account, although a common thread in the observer and journal accounts was that artillery played a significant role in the success of Japanese infantry attacks.[29] The effectiveness of artillery in reducing the

Russian defenses at Port Arthur and later in supporting infantry attacks at Mukden brought one observer to believe that the next war would an "artillery war."[30] Another observer believed that artillery would be the decisive arm in the next war, with all other arms subordinate to it.[31]

While an increased requirement for heavy artillery to reduce fortified defenses was a common lesson of the war, the fielding of heavy artillery (firing shells greater than 150-millimeter in diameter) was lacking by the Allied powers. Britain and France both started World War I with almost no medium or heavy artillery systems to support their infantry. Only Germany started the war with a significant number of large caliber guns, with sixteen 150-millimeter guns assigned to each corps.[32]

The use of indirect fire versus direct fire by artillery was another lesson from the Russo-Japanese War that varied by country. At Port Arthur and again at Mukden, the Japanese brought mountain guns and light artillery into their led trenches to suppress Russian defenses as its infantry advanced.[33] In support of these small bore guns the Japanese also used larger caliber artillery, moving it forward to within 450 yards of the enemy trenches.[34] This combined firepower, which also integrated hand grenades and trench mortar systems, usually resulted in a successful Japanese attack. While this close integration of firepower was recorded in several journal and observer accounts, many countries preferred to use its artillery in an indirect fire role only, with forward observers controlling fire by telephone.

The United States in its accounts felt that one of the primary artillery lessons of the war was the necessity of indirect versus direct fire artillery.[35] The French also considered indirect fires as a key element in modern artillery, and preferred to deploy its artillery in defilade positions or hidden behind hills or in wooded areas.[36] Artillery theorists in both Germany and Britain initially disagreed on whether direct or indirect fire was the best use of artillery. While both countries agreed that long-range fire support from covered positions was effective, discussions continued on the necessity of direct fire weapons.[37]

To bridge the gap between direct and indirect fire artillery, Germany went to war in 1914 with trained artillery liaison officers attached to forward infantry units to control its artillery. Britain followed a similar course of action and attempted to connect all front line units to its supporting artillery by telephone. Even with these dedicated communication lines, however, British infantry still had to cross the last 400 meters of any attack without indirect fires due to the inaccurate bursting radius of British artillery ordinance.[38]

After the beginning of World War I, both the Allied and Central Powers continued to wrestle with the concept of developing a mobile artillery platform to overcome the stalemate of trench warfare. The Allies eventually developed the tank as a mobile firepower system. Germany looked at other options, including the attachment of horse drawn artillery to front line infantry regiments.[39]

The final weapon system that will be discussed in this paper is the machinegun. The effectiveness of the machinegun was confirmed in almost every observer and journal accounts of the war. In one post war analysis, half of the total casualties were attributed to machinegun fires.[40] The use of the machinegun in an offensive role, however, was less apparent in the post-war accounts. While the Russian did use the machinegun to great effect in the defense, the Japanese were successful in using the weapon in numerous attacks at both Port Arthur and Mukden.

The accounts that discuss the use of the machinegun in an offensive role recommended that the weapon advance early in the attack to provide suppressive fire to advancing infantry.[41] To better support the use of the machinegun in an offensive role, several post-war journal accounts recommended that future machineguns be built to allow easier movement by hand (like the Japanese weapon), versus the heavier crew served Maxim Machineguns used by the Russians.[42] Whether in the offense or defense, the machinegun was a proven asset in the Russo-Japanese War. At the close of the conflict, Russia had increased its total inventory to over 800 machineguns.[43] Japan ended the war with 320 machineguns, with three to six assigned to each infantry regiment.[44]

While the utility of the machinegun was demonstrated in nearly every battle during the Russo-Japanese War, development of the weapon systems in the years prior to 1914 varied greatly due to costs and lack of doctrine for their employment.[45] Several journals published after the war recommended that twelve to sixteen machineguns be assigned to every division.[46] Germany took the lead in fielding machineguns units, and by October 1905, had sixteen six-gun detachments in service.[47]

Other nations debated the size machinegun elements to be developed and also at what level these elements should be assigned. Britain decided to maintain its two-gun section per battalion ratio that it established in 1905. France and Russia began fielding one machinegun section to each regiment of infantry.[48] The United States' observers were perhaps the least impressed with the role of the machinegun. One observer, who published a special report on the weapon after the war, stated "(that) the machine gun played a useful but not great part in the war."[49] This report stated that the machinegun should "not be kept in the firing line, but held in reserve until the opportune moment arrives."[50] The influence of this report on the U.S. Army is not known, but it was not until February of 1908, that the U.S. fielded its first provisional machinegun company and began to develop its doctrine.[51]

The total number of machineguns fielded by the major powers at the beginning of World War I varied. Germany, the leader in developing the weapon, had over 4,900 machineguns in 1914. France began the war with approximately 2,500 machineguns, and Britain entered the war with just 108 assigned to its initial BEF contingent.[52] When the United States entered the war three years later, a total of 1,453 machineguns were on hand, with 4,000 more on order from manufacturers.[53]

Many of the weapons that proved deadly on the 1914 European battlefield were clearly demonstrated during the Russo-Japanese War. While several countries had military observers on hand to record the events of the war, the massed casualties caused by hand grenades, mortars, artillery, and machineguns still shocked much of the world in the battles of World War I.

In preparing for the next war, most of the belligerent nations prepared for what they thought would be a battle of maneuver, based on philosophy of the offensive. Few nations expected that the next war would turn into a siege warfare battlefield that caused tens of thousands of casualties in a single day's action. Instead of trench warfare, nations expected the next battlefield to follow the lines of Mukden, with massed maneuvering forces.

The lessons gained from the trench fighting that took place at Port Arthur and along the southern lines of Mukden were discounted or even ignored by the militaries of the world. Many nations viewed the lessons observed during the Russo-Japanese War as tentative, believing that battles on the European landscape would be different. Others discounted the training and doctrine used by the combatants, even though both were trained on European standards.

Many of the tactical lessons of the Russo-Japanese War were lost as the world proceeded into World War I and what became a total war for many nations. Had the capabilities of these weapon systems been better understood prior to the 1914, doctrine and training could have changed the opening battles and perhaps reshaped history.

---

[1] Cited in Bruce Gudmundsson, *Stormtroop Tactics: Innovation in the German Army, 1914-1918* (New York: Praeger Publishers, 1989), 27.

[2] Alfred Vagts, *The Military Attaché* (Princeton: Princeton University Press, 1967), 261.

[3] The Russian leadership took offense to the departure of the observers and felt observers regarded the outlook for the Russian Army as hopeless. Ibid., 262-263.

[4] See *The Russo-Japanese War, Reports from the British Officers Attached to the Japanese Forces in the Field,* vol. 3 (London: Eyre and Spottiswoode, 1908).

[5] See *Conferences on the Russo-Japanese War* (Paris: Charles Lavauzelle, 1907) and *Der Russisch-Japanisch Krieg* (Berlin: Ernst Siegfried Mittler und Sohn, 1911); This account was also translated into Italian and Japanese. Menning, 201.

[6] Volume III of this account was completed in June 1914, but was not sent to the publishers until after the end of World War I. See *Official History of the Russo-Japanese War (Naval and Military),* vol. 3 (London: Wyman and Sons, Ltd., 1920).

[7] The Austria-Hungary account is not a General Staff account, but is a comprehensive account of the war. See War Department, Officer of the Chief of Staff, *Epitome of the Russo-Japanese War* (Washington: Government Printing Officer, 1907)

and Adolf Horsetzky, *An Epitome of the Russo-Japanese War of 1904-1905,* trans. Harry Bell. (Vienna: Seidel and Son, 1915; Fort Leavenworth: Army Services School, 1916).

[8]Greenwood, 113-114; Two other Italian observers, Fillippo Camperio and Luigi Giannitrapani, wrote extensive overviews of the war. Camperio wrote from the Russian side of the war up to the peace agreement in September 1905, while Giannitrapani wrote a balanced review of the war. See Fillippo Camperio, *In the Russian Camp in Manchuria*, trans. Victoria Kreuter, n.d., Special Collections, Combined Arms Research Library, Fort Leavenworth, Kansas. and Luigi Giannitrapani, *The Russo-Japanese War*, vol. 2, Translated by Frank Harris, 1907, Special Collections, Combined Arms Research Library, Fort Leavenworth, Kansas.

[9]Greenwood, 114-115.

[10]David Hermann, *The Arming of Europe and the Making of the First World War* (Princeton: Princeton University Press, 1996), 22-23, 28.

[11]Dupuy, *The Evolution of Weapons and Warfare,* 318.

[12]Greenwood, 2-3.

[13]See H. Cox, "A Lecture on the Some Moral Aspects of Modern War," *The Journal of the United Service Institution of India* 175 (April 1909), 151; "Precis of Foreign Military Papers," *The Journal of the United Service Institution of India* 175 (April 1909), 250; G. Orr (Captain), "Some Moral Factors in War," *The Journal of the United Service Institution of India* 180 (July 1910), 407; Walter Braithwaite (Brigadier General), "For the Conduct of an Army Character Weighs More than Knowledge or Service," *The Journal of the United Service Institution of India* 193 (April 1913): 351-352; Major H. Senior, "Precis of Foreign Military Papers," *The Journal of the United Service Institution of India* 163 (April 1906): 196; General De Negrier, "The Moral of Troops," *The Journal of the Royal United Service Institution* 333 (November 1905): 1295-1302; General De Negrier, "The Moral of Troops," *The Journal of the Royal United Service Institution* 334 (December 1905), 1426-1435; "Infantry Combat in the Russo-Japanese War," Translated from *Revue Militaire Des Armees Etrangerese* in *The Journal of the Royal United Service Institution* 344 (October 1906): 1274-1276; Greenwood, 436-437.

[14]Brigadier General J. Edmonds, *Military Operations, France and Belgium, 1914* (London: Macmillan and Co., Limited, 1922), 8-9.

[15]Colonel Breitkopf, "The Attack over Level Ground, In Conformity with German Drill Regulations of 1906," *Beiheft zum Militar-Wochenblatt* (1908), trans. A. Eisenberg in *Journal of the United States Infantry Association* 4 (January 1909): 585-588; and Gudmundsson, 21-22.

[16]Captain George Baltzell, "Some Impressions and Deduction Concerning the Company of Infantry in the Attack," *Journal of the United States Infantry Association* 2

(October 1906), 88-107; Captain H. Drum, "Collective Fire in Target Practice," *Journal of the United States Infantry Association* 3 (November 1907), 349-369; Captain George Baltzell, "The Proper Training of an Infantry Company," *Journal of the United States Infantry Association* 5 (March 1909): 639-663; Lieutenant Colonel K. Evans, "Infantry Fire in Battle," *Journal of the United States Infantry Association* 6 (May 1909): 820-853.

[17]Hermann, 99. The diversity of languages and cultures within the Austria-Hungary Empire probably had something to do with the regimented training style of that country.

[18]Arnold, CR3.5-7.

[19]De Negrier, "Some Lessons from the Russo-Japanese War," *Journal of the Royal United Service Institution* 341 (July 1906): 919.

[20]At Mukden, the Japanese used a grenade with a metal head and a wooden shaft, similar to a World War I German stick grenade. Bortnovski, 919-920; P. Cleator, *Weapons of War* (New York: Thomas Y. Crowell Company, 1967), 174.

[21]*Official History of the Russo-Japanese War,* part 3, 169, 229.

[22]"Hand and Rifle Grenades," 916.

[23]Edmonds, 10-11, 398.

[24]The Royal Engineers used gun cotton as the explosive and discarded tin cans for the body of its early grenades. Ibid., 398; Cleator, 174.

[25]Both British and Russian journal articles discounted the utility of the trench mortar due to accuracy and explosive power of the charge. The Russian article, cited below, was re-published in a French military journal and U.S. artillery journal. See Colonel Neznamov, "Teachings of the Russo-Japanese War," *Journal des Sciences Militaires* (March 1906), translated by William Lassiter in *Journal of the United States Artillery* 3 (May-June 1906): 299; W. Carey, "The Experience of the Russo-Japanese War," *The Journal of the United Service Institution of India* 165 (October 1906): 428; Captain Ashely Barrett, "Lessons to be Learned by Regimental Officers from the Russo-Japanese War," *The Journal of the Royal United Service Institution* 353 (July 1907), 807.

[26]By November 1918, the United States had produced 2390 trench mortars varying in caliber from 3-inch to 9.45-inches. France's first purpose built mortar was the Mortar '58 cal. No. 1, developed in 1915. Benedict Crowell, *America's Munitions 1917-1918* (Washington: Government Printing Office, 1919), 211-212, 217; Philip Haythornthwaite, *World War One: 1915* (London: Arms and Armour Press, 1989), plate 26.

[27]Gudmundsson, 34-35, 80-81.

[28]*Handbook of the German Army in War, April 1918* (Nashville: The Battery Press, Inc., 1996), 102-105.

[29]Horn, 257; Greenwood, 426-427; Fuller, *A Military History of the Western World*, 167-169; and *Reports of Military Observers Attached to the Armies in Manchuria During the Russo-Japanese War,* part 3, 220-221.

[30]Birnie, 201.

[31]Another British observer stated that artillery would be the decisive arm in the future. *The Russo-Japanese War, Reports from the British Officers Attached to the Japanese Forces in the Field,* vol. 3, 209, 117.

[32]France began the war predominately armed with 75mm guns. In 1914, France had just began to field its 105mm Schneider Howitzers, with 84 available at the start of the war. Antulio Echevarria, *After Clausewitz, German Military Thinkers Before the Great War* (Lawrence: University Press of Kansas, 2000), 146; Edmonds, 10-11; Herrmann, 90-92; and Frank Comparato, *Age of Great Guns* (Harrisburg: The Stackpole Company, 1965), 118.

[33]Major K. Knapp, "The Tactical Employment of Pack Artillery," *The Journal of the Royal United Service Institution* 336 (February 1905), 199; *Reports of Military Observers Attached to the Armies in Manchuria During the Russo-Japanese War,* part 3, 58, 158, and 219; Niessel, 124; *Official History (Naval and Military) of the Russo-Japanese War,* vol. 2, 73; Nogine, 286; "The Von Lobell Annual Reports on the Changes and Progress in Military Matters in 1905," 1391; Reichmann, 4; and Sedgwick, *The Russo-Japanese War, A Sketch*, 191.

[34]*The Russo-Japanese War, Reports from the British Officers Attached to the Japanese Forces in the Field,* Vol. 2, 366; Hossfeld, "The Russo-Japanese War," 250.

[35]*Reports of the Military Observers to the Armies in Manchuria During the Russo-Japanese War,* part 1, 280.

[36]Herrmann, 80-81.

[37]Ibid., 88; Echevarria, 147-148.

[38]Echevarria, 146 and endnote number 52 on page 268.

[39]Timothy Lupfer, *The Dynamics of Doctrine, the Changes in German Tactical Doctrine During the First World War* (Fort Leavenworth: Combat Studies Institute, 1981), 38, 42.

[40]Dolf Goldsmith, *The Devil's Paintbrush, Sir Hiram Maxim's Gun,* ed. R. Stevens (Toronto: Collector Grade Publications, Inc., 1993), 141.

[41] Reilly, 801-802; Captain F. Keen, "Machine Guns," *The Journal of the United Service Institution of India* 176 (July 1909), 457-458; *The Russo-Japanese War, Reports from the British Officers Attached to the Japanese Forces in the Field,* vol. 2, 346.

[42] Neznamov, 301; "Military Notes, 1333; "Professional Notes, Lessons of the Russo-Japanese War: Armament," *Journal of the United States Artillery* 2 (September-October 1905): 173.

[43] Herrmann, 68.

[44] "The Present Status of the Equipment of the Armies of the World with Machine-guns," *Beheft 79 zur Internationalen Revue uber die gesamten Armeen und Flotten* (October 1906), trans. Oliver Spaulding, *Journal of the United States Infantry Association* 1 (July 1906): 157; Captain H. Hale, "Infantry: Organization, Equipment and Training," *Journal of the United States Infantry Association* 1 (July 1906), 32; Niessell, 102.

[45] Herrmann, 68-70.

[46] See "Military Notes," 1333; "Professional Notes, Lessons of the Russo-Japanese War: Armament," 173; Neznamov, 301; and Carey, "The Experience of the Russo-Japanese War," 429.

[47] "The Present Status of the Equipment of the Armies of the World with Machine-guns," 147.

[48] Roger Ford, *The Grim Reaper, the Machine-gun and Machine-gunners* (London: Sidgwick & Jackson, 1996), 95; Herrmann, 69; "Precis of Foreign Military Papers, Russian Papers," *The Journal of the United Service Institution of India* 178 (January 1910): 180.

[49] Greenwood, 446. The special report was written for the U.S. Military Information Division of the General Staff and later published in the Journal of the United States Cavalry. See Lieutenant Colonel Montgomery Macomb, "Machine guns in the Russian Army During the Campaign in Manchuria, 1904-1905," *Journal of the U.S. Cavalry Association* 3 (January 1907): 443-452.

[50] Macomb, "Machine guns in the Russian Army During the Campaign in Manchuria, 1904-1905," 449.

[51] Captain John Parker, "Progress in Machine Gun Development," *Journal of the United States Infantry Association* 1 (July 1908), 3.

[52] Lieutenant Colonel G. Hutchison, *Machine Gun, The History and Tactical Employment* (London: Macmillian and Company, Ltd., 1938), 97; Ford, 94-95.

[53]Crowell, 161.

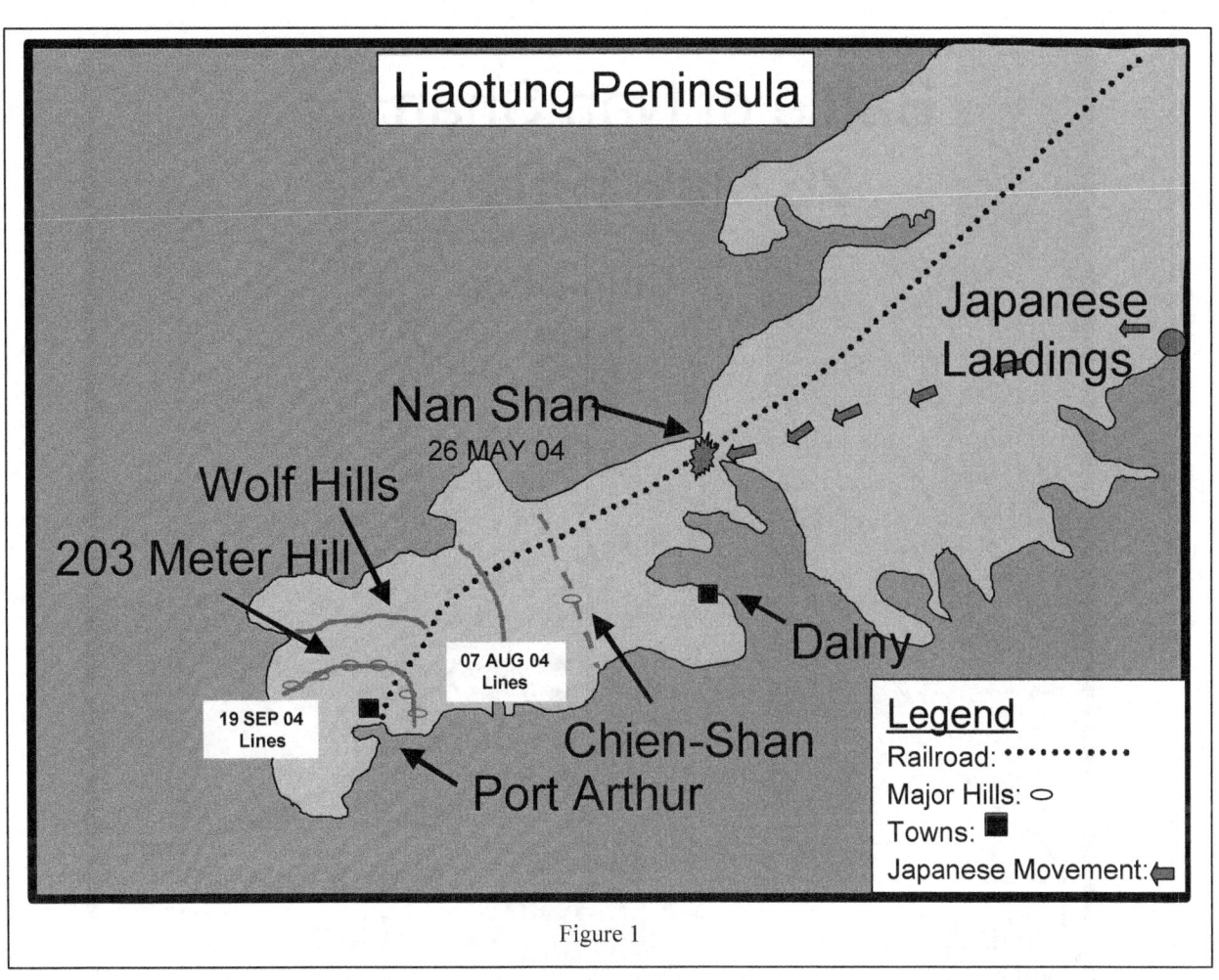

Figure 1

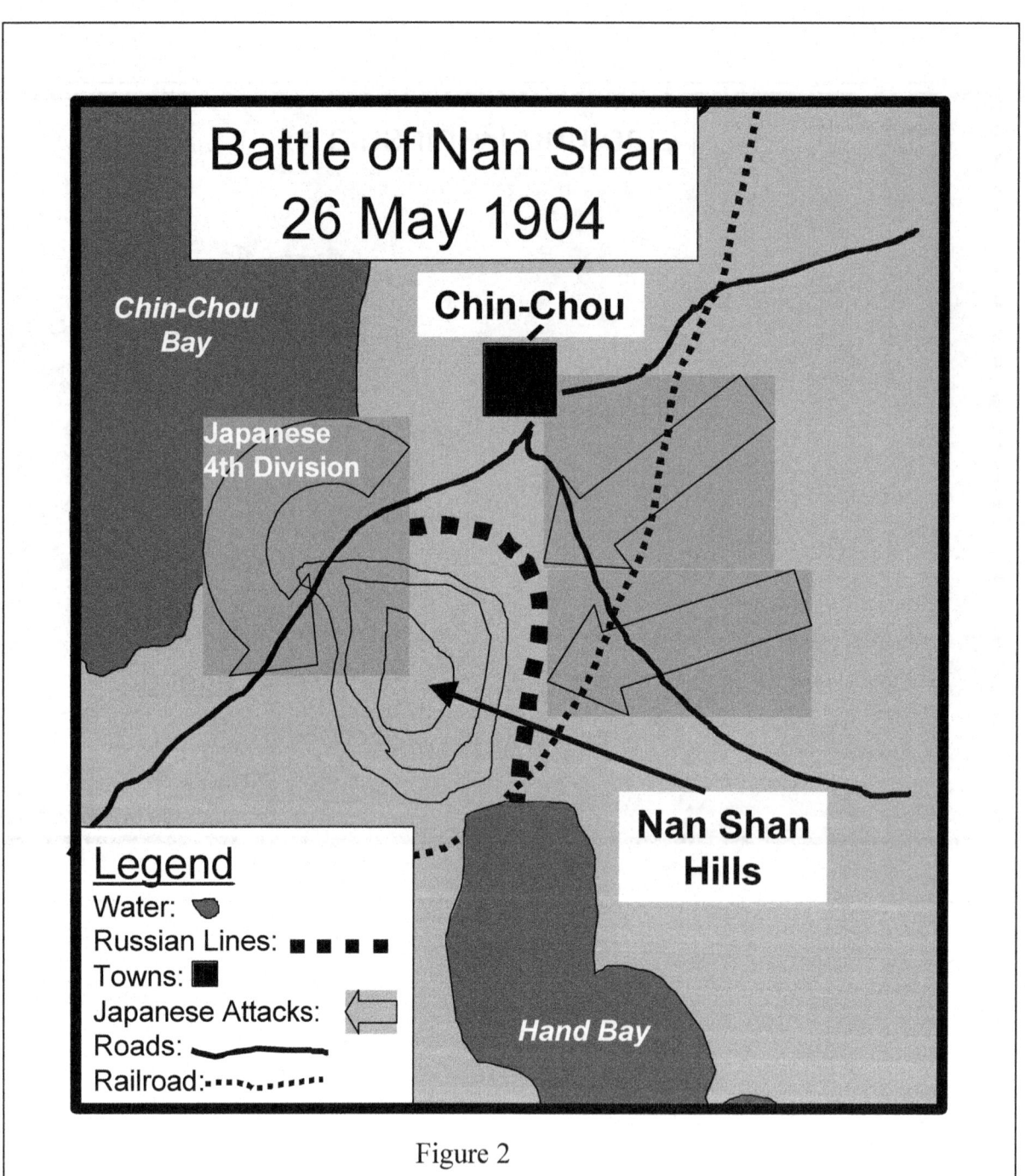

Figure 2

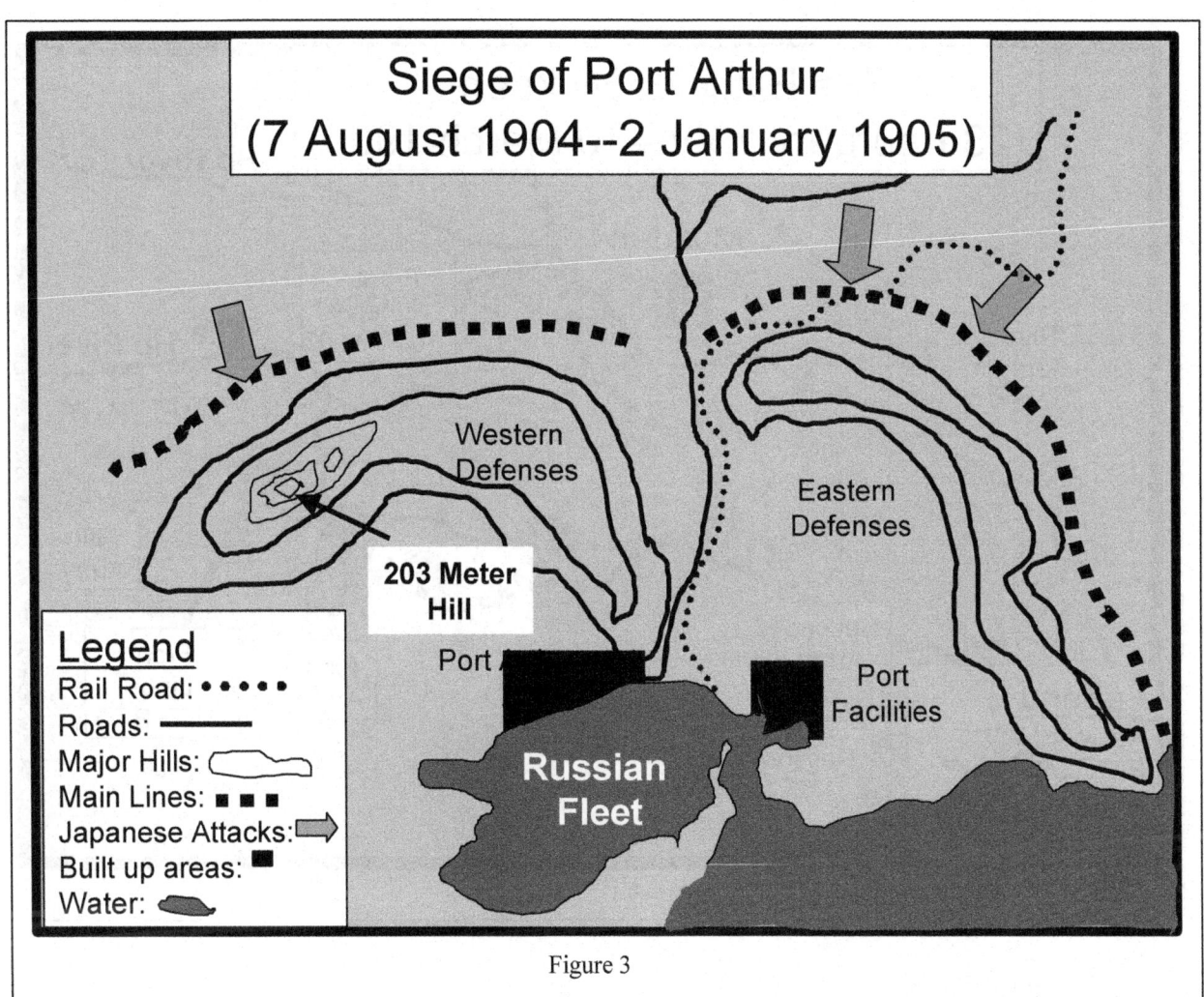

Figure 3

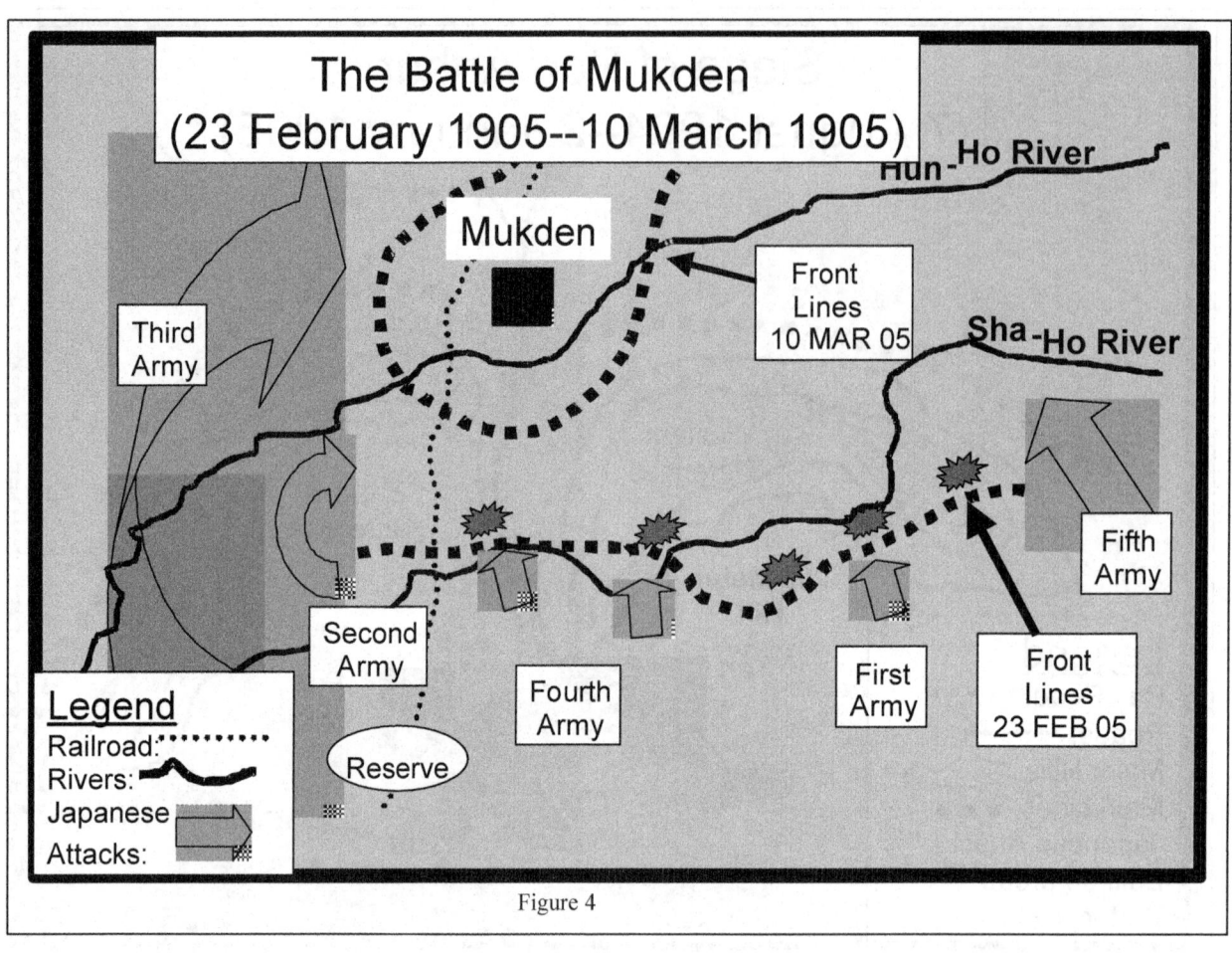

Figure 4

BIBLIOGRAPHY

Books

Addington, Larry. The Patterns of War Since the Eighteenth Century. 2d ed. Bloomington: Indiana University Press, 1994.

Anderson, J. *The Russo-Japanese War on Land, 1904-1905, up to the Battle of Liao-Yang.* London, Hugh Rees, Ltd., 1909.

Arnold, Joseph. "French Tactical Doctrine, 1870-1914," *Military Affairs* (April 1978): 61-67. Reprinted in U.S. Army Command and General Staff College, *I085 Critical Reasoning and I503 Leader Assessment an Development Readings Book.* Fort Leavenworth: USACGSC (August 2002), CR3.5-1--CR3.5-10.

Asakawa, K. *The Russo-Japanese Conflict: Its Causes and Issues.* Boston: Houghton Mifflin Company, 1904.

Ashmead-Bartlett, Ellis. *Port Arthur, The Siege and Capitulation.* 2nd ed. Edinburgh: William Blackwood and Sons, 1906.

Asiaticus. Translated by J. Montgomery. *Reconnaissance in the Russo-Japanese War.* London: Hugh Rees, Ltd., 1908.

Barry, Richard. *Port Arthur: A Monster Heroism.* New York: Moffat, Yard andCompany, 1905.

Beasley, W. *Japanese Imperialism, 1894-1945.* Oxford; New York: Clarendon Press, 1987.

Bell, William. *Commanding General and Chiefs of Staff, 1775-1983.* Washington D.C.: Center of Military History, 1983.

Birnie, Arthur. *The Art of War.* London: Thomas Nelson and Sons, Ltd., 1942.

Brooke, Leopold. *An Eye-Witness in Manchuria.* London: Eveleigh Nash, 1905.

Camperio, Fillippo, *In the Russian Camp in Manchuria.* Translated by Victoria Kreuter, n.d., Special Collections, Combined Arms Research Library, Fort Leavenworth, Kansas.

Cleator, P. *Weapons of War.* New York: Thomas Y. Crowell Company, 1967.

Clausewitz, Carl von. *On* War. Edited and translated by Michael Howard and Peter Paret. Princeton: Princeton University Press, 1984.Collier's War Correspondents. *The Russo-Japanese War.* New York: P. F. Collier and Son, 1905.

Committee of Imperial Defense. *Official History of the Russo-Japanese War.* Part 1. London: Harrison and Sons, 1909.

Committee of Imperial Defense. *Official History of the Russo-Japanese War.* Part 3. London: Harrison and Sons, 1909.

Committee of Imperial Defense. *Official History (Naval and Military) of the Russo-Japanese War.* Vol. 2. London: Wyman and Sons, Ltd., 1912.

Committee of Imperial Defense. *Official History (Naval and Military) of the Russo-Japanese War.* Vol. 3. London: Wyman and Sons, Ltd., 1920.

Comparato, Frank. *Age of Great Guns.* Harrisburg: The Stackpole Company, 1965.

Connaughton, R. The War of the Rising Sun and Tumbling Bear: A History of the Russo-Japanese War 1905-1906. London: Routledge, 1988.

Corbett, Julian. *Maritime Operations in the Russo-Japanese War, 1904-1905,* Vol. 1. Maryland: Naval Institute Press, 1994.

Cordonnier, E. *The Japanese in Manchuria 1904.* Vol. 2. Translated by C. Atkinson. London: Hugh Rees Ltd., 1914.

Coffman, Edward. The War to End all Wars, The American Military Experience in World War I. Madison: The University of Wisconsin Press, 1986.

Crowell, Benedict. *America's Munitions 1917-1918.* Washington: Government Printing Office, 1919.

De Négrier, General. *Lessons of the Russo-Japanese War.* London: Hugh Rees, Ltd., 1906.

Donat, Karl. *The Battle of Mukden.* London: Hugh Rees, Ltd., 1906.

Dupuy, Ernest, and Trevor Dupuy. *The Encyclopedia of Military History, from 3500 B.C. to Present.* Rev. ed. New York: Harper & Row, 1977.

Dupuy, Trevor. *The Evolution of Weapons and Warfare.* Fairfax: Hero Books, 1984.

Earle, Edward, ed. Makers *of Modern Strategy.* Princeton, Princeton University Press, 1973.

Edmonds, J., Brigadier General. *Military Operations, France and Belgium, 1914.* London: Macmillan and Co., Ltd., 1922.

Echevarria II, Antulio. After Clausewitz: German Military Thinkers Before theGreat War. Lawrence: University of Kansas, 2000.English, John, and Bruce Gudmundsson. *On Infanry.* Rev. Ed., Westport: Praeger, 1994.

Falls, Cyril. *A Hundred Years of War, 1850-1950.* 3rd ed. New York: Collier Books, 1967.

Footsloger (pseudonym). *A Short Account of the Russo-Japanese War.* London: Forster Groom & Co., Ltd., 1925.

Ford, Roger. *The Grim Reaper: The Machine-gun and Machine-gunners.* London: Sidgwick and Jackson, 1996.

Fraser, David. A Modern Campaign, or War and Wireless Telegraphy in the Far East. London: Methuen & Co., 1905.

Fuller, J. *A Military History of the Western World.* Vol. 3. New York: Funk and Wagnalls Company, Inc., 1956.

_____. The Conduct of War 1789-1961. New York: Da Capo Press, 1992.

German General Staff. Pamphlet 37-38, Individual Contributions to the History of *Wars, Port Arthur.* Translated by Paul Brockmann. Berlin: Ernst SiegfriedVittler & Son, 1906; Fort Leavenworth: Combined Arms Research Library, Special Collections, 1907.

German Official Account of the Russo-Japanese War, Between San-de-pu and Mukden. Translated by Karl Donat, London: Hugh Rees Ltd., 1913.

German Official Account of the Russo-Japanese War, The Battle of Mukden, Part 1. Translated by Karl Donat. London: Hugh Rees Ltd., 1914.

German Official Account of the Russo-Japanese War, The Ya-Lu. Translated by Karl Donat. London: Hugh Rees Ltd., 1908.

German Official Account of the Russo-Japanese War, Wa-Fan-Gou and Actions Preliminary to Liao-Han. Translated by Karl Donat. London: Hugh Rees Ltd., 1908.

German Official Account of the Russo-Japanese War, Yin-Kou and San-De-Pu. Translated by Karl Donat. London: Hugh Rees Ltd., 1910.

Giannitrapani, Luigi, *The Russo-Japanese War*. Vol. 2. Translated by FrankHarris, Special Collections, Combined Arms Research Library, Fort Leavenworth, Kansas, 1907.

Goldsmith, Dolf. *The Devil's Paintbrush: Sir Hiram Maxim's Gun.* Edited by R. Stevens. Toronto: Collector Grade Publications, Ltd., 1993

Greenwood, John. "The American Military Observers of the Russo-Japanese War (1904-1905)." Ph.D. diss., Kansas State University, 1971. Griffith, Paddy. *Forward into Battle, Fighting Tactics from Waterloo to Vietnam.* London: Anthony Bird Publications, 1981.

Gudmundsson, Bruce. Stormtroop Tactics, Innovation in the German Army, 1914-1918. New York: Praeger Publishing, 1989.

Hamiliton, Ian. *A Staff Officer's Scrap-Book: During the Russo-Japanese War.* London: Edward Arnold, 1905.*Handbook of the German Army in War, April 1918.* Nashville: The Battery Press, 1996.

Hargreaves, Reginald. *Red Sun Rising: The Siege of Port Arthur.* Philadelphia: J. B.Lippincott, 1962.

Harries, Meirion and Susie Harries. Soldiers of the Sun: The Rise and Fall of the Imperial Japanese Army. New York: Random House, 1991.

Haythornthwaite, Philip. *World War One: 1915.* London: Arms and Armor Press, 1989.

_____. *World War One: 1917.* London: Arms and Armor Press, 1990.

Herrmann, David. *The Arming of Europe and the Making of the First World War.* Princeton: Princeton University Press, 1996.

Horsetzky, Adolf. *An Epitome of the Russo-Japanese War of 1904-1905.* Translated by Harry Bell. Vienna: Seidel & Son, 1915; Fort Leavenworth: Army Services Schools, 1916.

Howard, Michael. "Men Against Fire, Expectations of War in 1914." *International Security* (summer 1984): 41-57. Reprinted in *I085 Critical Reasoning and I503 Leader Assessment and Development Readings Book.* Fort Leavenworth: USACGSC (August 2002), CR3.8-1--CR3.8-11.

_____. *War in European History.* Oxford: Oxford University Press, 1976.

Kinai, M. *The Russo-Japanese War (Official Reports).* Vol. 1. London: Kegan Paul, Trench, Taubner and Company, Ltd., n.d.

_____. *The Russo-Japanese War (Official Reports).* Vol. 2. London: Kegan Paul, Trench, Taubner and Company, Ltd., n.d.

Kuropatkin, Alexei. *The Russian Army and the Japanese War.* Vol. 1. Translated by A. Lindsay and edited by E. Swinton. New York: E. P. Dutton, 1909.

Kuropatkin, Alexei. *The Russian Army and the Japanese War.* Vol. 2. Translated by A. Lindsay and edited by E. Swinton. New York: E. P. Dutton, 1909. Liddell Hart, B. *The Real War, 1914-1918.* Boston: Little, Brown and Company, 1964. Lone, Stewart. *Japan's First Modern War.* London: St. Martin's Press, 1994.

Maxwell, William. *From the Yalu to Port Arthur.* London: Hutchinson and Co., 1906.

Menning, Bruce. Bayonets Before Bullets: The Imperial Russian Army, 1861-1914. Bloomington: Indiana University Press, 1992.

Nojine, K. *The Truth about Port Arthur.* Translated by A. Lindsay and edited by E. Swinton. New York: Dutton and Company, 1908.

Norregaard, B. The Great Siege, The Investment and Fall of Port Arthur. London: Methuen and Co., 1906.

Okamoto, Shumpei. *The Japanese Oligarchy and the Russo-Japanese War.* New York: Columbia University Press, 1970.

Peattie, Mark. *Ishiwara Kanji and Japan's Confrontation with the West.* Princeton: Princeton University Press, 1975.

Perret, Geoffrey. *Old Soldiers Never Die.* New York: Random House, 1996.

Porter, Robert. *Japan, The Rise of a Modern Power.* Oxford: The Clarendon Press, 1919.

Presseisen, Ernst. *Before Aggression: Europeans Prepare the Japanese Army.* Tucson: University of Arizona, 1965.

Ross, Charles, Colonel. *An Outline of the Russo-Japanese War 1904,1905.* Vol. 1. London: Macmillan and Co., Ltd., 1912.

Rowan-Robinson, H. *The Campaign of Liao-Yang.* London: Constable and Company, Ltd., 1914.

Ruckman, John. The Command and Administration of the Fortress of Port Arthur During the Russo-Japanese War. Reprinted from Journal of United States Artillery (November- December 1915), n.d.

The Russo-Japanese War, Reports from British Officers Attached to the Japanese Forces in the Field. Vol. 1. London: General Staff, 1907.

_____. Vol. 2. London: General Staff, 1908.

Ryan, J. *Guns, Mortars and Rockets.* Oxford; New York: Brassey's Publishing Limited, 1982.

Sakurai, Tadayoshi. *Human Bullets: A Soldier's Story of Port Arthur.* Translated by Masujiro Honda and edited by Alice Bacon. Boston: Houghton, Mifflin and *Company*, 1907.

Sedgwick, F. The Campaign in Manchuria 1904-1905: Second Period--The Decisive Battles. London: George Allen and Company, Ltd., 1912.

_____. *The Russo-Japanese War, A Sketch.* London: Swan Sonnenschein & Co., 1909.

Soloviev, L. Actual Experiences in War: Battle Acton of the Infantry; Impressions of a Company Commander. Washington D.C.: War Department, 1906.

Travers, T. "Technology, Tactics, and Morale: Jean de Bloch, the Boer War, and British *Military* Theory, 1900-1914." *Journal of Modern History* 51 (June 1979): 264-86. *Reprinted* in U.S. Army Commmand and General Staff College, *I085 Critical Reasoning and I503 Leader Assessment an Development Readings Book.* Fort Leavenworth: USACGSC (August 2002), CR3.7-1--CR3.7-14

Tettau, *Freihen*, Trans. *Port Arthur, The Authorized German Translation from the*

Russian General Staff Account, Vol. 5, *Part* I. Translated (to English) by Walter

Buttgenbach. Berlin: Unknown, *1910*; *Special* Collections, Fort Leavenworth: Combined Arms Research Library, *1912*.

_____. Port Arthur, The Authorized German Translation from the Russian General Staff Account, Vol. V, Part II. Translated (to English) by Walter Buttgenbach. Berlin: Unknown, *1910*; Special Collections, Fort Leavenworth: Combined Arms Research Library, *1912*.

Tretyakov, N. My Experiences with at Nan Shan and Port Arthur with the Fifth Siberian Rifles. Translated by A. Alford and edited by F. Baker. London: Hugh Rees, Ltd., 1911

Turabian, Kate. *A Manual for Writers of Term Papers, Theses, and Dissertations.* 6th ed. Chicago: University of Chicago Press, 1996.

Veresaev, V. *In the War. Translated* by Leo Wiener. New York: Michell Kennerley, 1917.

Villiers, Frederic. *Port Arthur, Three Months with the Besiegers.* London: Longmans, Green, and Co., 1905.

Walder, *David. The Short Victorious War.* 1st ed. New York: Harper and Row, 1973.

War Department. Office of the Chief of Staff. *Epitome of the Russo-Japanese War.* Part 1. *Washington*: Government Printing Office, 1906.

_____. *Reports of Military Observers Attached to the Armies in Manchuria During the Russo-Japanese War.* Part 1. Washington: Government Printing Office, 1906.

_____. Reports of Military Observers Attached to the Armies in Manchuria During the Russo-Japanese War. Part 2--3. Washington: Government Printing Office, 1906.

_____. *Reports of Military Observers Attached to the Armies in Manchuria During the Russo-Japanese War.* Part 4. Washington: Government Printing Office, 1907.

_____. Reports of Military Observers Attached to the Armies in Manchuria During the Russo-Japanese War. Part 5. Washington: Government Printing Office, 1907.

Warner, Denis, and Peggy Warner. *The Tide at Sunrise: A History of the Russo-JapaneseWar, 1904-1905.* New York: Charterhouse, 1974.

Wood, Oliver. *From the Yalu to Port Arthur.* Kansas City: Franklin Hudson Publishing Co., 1905.

Periodicals and Articles (Service Journals)

Archdale, T. "Three Weeks in Manchuria." *The Journal of the United Service Institution of India* 168 (July 1907): 277-296

Aspinall, C. "Interior or Exterior Lines?" *The Journal of the United Services Institution of India* 176 (July 1909): 301-306.

Aubert, Captain. "The Russian Cavalry at Mukden." *Kavalleristische Monatshefte,* Translated by Harry Bell in *Journal of U.S. Cavalry Association* 63 (April 1908): 745-754.

Badham-Thornhill, R. "How Japan makes her Army Officer." *Journal of U.S. Cavalry Association* 57 (July 1905): 111-115.

Baltzell, George, Captain. "The Proper Training of an Infantry Company." *Journal of the United States Infantry Association* 5 (March 1909): 639-663.

_____. "Some Impressions and Deduction Concerning the Company of Infantry in the Attack." *Journal of the United States Infantry Association* 2 (October 1906): 88-108.

Barnes, John. "Theater of War." *Journal of the United States Infantry Association* 4(January 1908): 589-607.

Barrett, Ashley. "Lessons to be Learned by Regimental Officers from the Russo-Japanese War." *The Journal of the Royal United Service Institution* 353 (July 1907): 797-823.

Bingham, W., Captain. "After Mukden: A Russian Verdict on Russian Failures." *TheJournal of the Royal United Service Institution* 328 (June 1905): 686-695.Bird, W., Lieutenant Colonel. "The Battle of Te-Li-ssu." *The Journal of the United Services Institution of India* 191 (April 1913): 153-178.

Black, Major. "The Intrenchment (sic) of Infantry During the Attack." *Internationale Revue uber die gesamten Armeen und Flotten,* Translated by Raymond Sheldon in Journal *of The United States Infantry Association* 2 (January 1907): 148-153.

_____. "Night Operations of the Japanese in 1904." Translated from *Militar-Wochenblatt* in *The Journal of the United Services Institution of India* 191 (April 1913): 197-217.

_____. "Tactics of Infantry 1903." Translated by Henry Hossfeld in *Journal of the United States Infantry Association* 3, (January 1905): 144-163.

_____. "Tactics of Arms Combined." Translated by Henry Hossfeld in *Journal of the United States Infantry Association* 4 (April 1905): 89-104.

Bortnoviski, A. "Hand Grenades in the Russo-Japanese War." Translated from *Voiennyi Sbornick* in *The Journal of the Royal United Service Institution* 389 (July 1910): 918-922.

Braithwaite, Walter, Brigadier General. "For the Conduct of an Army Character Weighs More than Knowledge or Science." *The Journal of the United Service Institute of India* 193 (October 1913): 351-367.

Breitkopf, Colonel. "The Attack over Level Ground, In Conformity with German Drill Regulations of 1906." *Beiheft zum Militar-Wochenblatt* (1908). Translated by A. Eisenberg in *Journal of the United States Infantry Association* 4 (January 1909): 585-612.

Burton, R. "2nd Essay Bombay Command, 1904." *The Journal of the United Services Institution of India* 163 (April 1906): 124-134.

B., W. "Reflections on Russian Strategy in Manchuria in 1904." *The Journal of the United Service Institution of India* 159 (April 1905): 172-192.

Cadell, J., Major. " Theories as to the Best Position for Quick-firing Shielded Field Artillery." The Journal of the Royal United Service Institution 346 (December 1906): 1475-1487.

Carey, W., Captain. "The Experience of the Russo-Japanese War." *The Journal of the United Service Institution of India* 165 (October 1906): 427-436.

_____. "Precis of Foreign Military Papers, Italian Papers." *The Journal of the United Service Institution of India* 163 (April 1906): 199-202.

"Changes in the Tendencies in the Russian Army Since the War Against Japan." *The Journal of the Royal United Service Institution* 393 (November 1910): 1446-1469.

Clarke, J. "The Struggle for the Pacific." extracted by the author from *Rene Pinon* in *The Journal of the Royal United Service Institution* 325 (March 1905): 293-299.

Cloman, Sidney. "The Circum-Baikal Railroad." *Journal of the United States Infantry Association* 2 (October 1906): 53-64.

_____. "The Decauville Horse Railroad with the Russian Army in Manchuria." *Journal of the United States Infantry Association* 3 (January 1907): 22-29.

Collins, C. "Lessons to be Learn from the Siege of Port Arthur as Regards to R.E. Work." *The Journal of the United Services Institution of India* 179 (April 1910): 297-311.

"Communications on the Battle-field." *La Revue d' Infanterie.* Extracted and translated by Lieutenant Colonel Frocard and Captain Painvin. *The Journal of the Royal United Service Institution* 373 (March 1909): 357-379.

Cox, H., Colonel. "A Lecture on Some Moral Aspects of Modern War." *The Journal of the United Services Institution of India* 175 (April 1909): 141-153.

Curtis, A. "The Siege of Port Arthur from a Naval Aspect." *The Journal of the Royal United Service Institution* 335 (January 1906): 43-86.

Degtyarev, A. "Notes Upon Company and Battalion Tactics and the Employment of Artillery in Battle. Based on the Experiences of the Russo-Japanese War of 1904-05." Part 1. Translated from *Voiennyi Sbornik* in *The Journal of the Royal United Service Institution* 359 (January 1908): 64-75.

_____. "Notes Upon Company and Battalion Tactics and the Employment of Artillery in Battle. Based on the Experiences of the Russo-Japanese War of 1904-05." Part 2. Translated from *Voiennyi Sbornik* in *The Journal of the Royal United Service Institution* 360 (February 1908): 331-344.

_____. "Notes Upon Company and Battalion Tactics and the Employment of Artillery in Battle. Based on the Experiences of the Russo-Japanese War of 1904-05." Part 3. Translated from *Voiennyi Sbornik* in *The Journal of the Royal United Service Institution,* 361 (March 1908): 224-235.

De Négrier, General. "The Moral of Troops." Translated from *Revue des Deux Mondes* in *Journal of the Royal United Service Institution* 334 (December 1905): 1426-1435.

_____. "The Moral of Troops." Translated from *Revue des Deux Mondes* in *Journal of the Royal United Service Institution* 333 (November 1905): 1295-1302.

_____. "Some Lessons from the Russo-Japanese War." *Journal of the Royal United Service Institution* 339 (May 1906): 687-698.

_____. "Some Lessons from the Russo-Japanese War." *Journal of the Royal United Service Institution* 341 (July 1906): 910-919.

Drum, H., Captain. "Collective Fire In Target Practice." *Journal of the United States Infantry Association* 3 (November 1907): 349-370.

Evans, R., Lieutenant Colonel. "Infantry Fire in Battle." *Journal of the United States Infantry Association* 6 (May 1909): 819-853.

Ewbank, W. "The Use of Field Fortifications." *The Journal of the United Service Institution of* India 163 (April 1906): 116-123.

Fendall, C. "Field Artillery, A Lecture." *The Journal of the United Services Institution of India* 162 (January 1906): 39-52.

Fraser, David. "Doings of Japanese Calvary." *Journal of U.S. Cavalry Association,* 58(October 1905): 319-325.

_____. "The Cavalry Lessons of the War." *Journal of U.S. Cavalry Association* 59 (January 1906): 484-494.

Giannitrappani, L., Captain. "Considerations on and Conclusions from the Siege of Port Arthur." *Rivista di Artiglieria e Genio* (December 1906), Translated by W. Carey in *The Journal of the United Service Institution of India* 169 (October 1907): 523-537.

_____. "The Operations Round Port Arthur in 1904. The Development of the Investment and Siege of the Fortress." *Rivista di Artiglieria e Genio* (November 1906), Translated by W. Carey in *The Journal of the United Service Institution of India* 168 (July 1907): 372-385.

_____. "The Operations Round Port Arthur in 1904. Three Lectures by Captain L. Giantrappani of the Italian Artillery." *Rivista di Artiglieria e Genio* (October 1906). Translated by W. Carey in *The Journal of the United Service Institution of India* 167 (April 1907): 259-269.

Gunter, E. "The Von Lobell Annual Reports on the Changes and Progress in Military Matters in 1903." *The Journal of the Royal United Service Institution,* 320 (October 1904): 1125-1163.

_____. "The Von Lobell Annual Reports on the Changes and Progress in MilitaryMatters in 1904." The Journal of the Royal United Service Institution 333 (November 1905): 1265-1284.

_____. "The Von Lobell Annual Reports on the Changes and Progress in Military Matters in 1904." The Journal of the Royal United Service Institution 334 (December 1905): 1393-1414.

_____. "The Von Lobell Annual Reports on the Changes and Progress in Military Matters in 1904," The Journal of the Royal United Service Institution 336 (February 1906): 225-230.

_____. "The Von Lobell Annual Reports on the Changes and Progress in Military Matters in 1904." The Journal of the Royal United Service Institution 337 (March 1906): 343-348.

_____. "The Von Lobell Annual Reports on the Changes and Progress in Military Matters in 1905." *The Journal of the Royal United Service Institution* 345 (November 1906): 1387-1400.

Hale, H. "Infantry: Organization, Equipment, Training." *Journal of the United States Infantry Association* 1 (July 1906): 30-52.

"Hand and Rifle Grenades." Translated from *Streffleures Oesterreichische Milit*arische Zeitschrift in The Journal of the Royal United Service Institution 401 (July 1911): 915-922.

Hawthorne, Harry. "Heavy Caliber Cannon in the Field." *Journal of the United States Artillery* 1 (March-April 1908): 137-151.

Horn, Tiemann. "Present Method and Lessons in Regard to Field Artillery Taught by the Russo-Japanese War." *Journal of the United States Artillery* 3 (November-December 1908): 251-262.

"Infantry Combat in the Russo-Japanese War." Translated from *Revue Militaire Des Armees* Etrangeres in *Journal of the Royal United Service Institution* 342 (August 1906): 1048-1053.

"Infantry Combat in the Russo-Japanese War (Part 2)." Translated from *Revue Militaire Des Armees Etrangeres* in *Journal of the Royal United Service Institution* 344 (October 1906): 1273-1280.

"The Japanese Infantry Attack." *Journal of the United States Infantry Association* 3(January 1905): 3-25.

Johnson, William, Major. "The Infantry Machine-gun Detachment," *Journal of the United States Infantry Association* 3 (November 1908): 391-408.

K, B. "Japanese Ruses of War." Translated from *Militar-Wochenblatt* 78 (June 1905) *The Journal of the Royal United Service Institution* 332 (October 1905): 1188-1190.

Keen, F., Captain. "Machine Guns." *The Journal of the United Services Institution of India* 176 (July 1909): 455-462.

Kernan, F., Major. "Selection Versus Seniority." Journal of the *United States Infantry Association* 5 (March 1909): 695-710.

Knapp, K. "The Tactical Employment of Pack Artillery." *The Journal of the UnitedService Institution of India* 336 (February 1905): 199-206.

Knox, H. "Reserves in the Russo-Japanese War." *The Journal of the United Services Institution of India* 193 (October 1913): 403-414.

Kirton, W. "With the Japanese on the Yalu." *The Journal of the Royal United Service Institution* 325 (March 1905): 269-286.

Kuhn, J. "From Port Arthur to Mukden with Nogi." *The Journal of the Royal United Service Institution* 340 (June 1906): 798-804.

"Machine Gun Fire." Translated from Leitfaden fur den Unterricht in der Waffenlehre in The Journal of the Royal United Service Institution, 401 (July 1911): 911-914.

Macomb, M., Major. "The Russian Infantry Soldier." *The Journal of the Royal United Service Institution* 342 (August 1906): 1013-1022.

Macomb, Montgomery. "Machine Guns in the Russian Army." *Journal of the United States Infantry Association* 3 (January 1907): 3-21.

Macomb, Montgomery. "Machine Guns in the Russian Army During the Campaign in Manchuria, 1904-1905." *Journal of U.S. Cavalry Association* 63 (January 1907): 443-452.

Macomb, Montgomery. "More about Machine Guns." *Journal of U.S. Cavalry Association* 64 (April 1907): 605-608.

McMahon, John. "Indirect Fire." *Journal of U.S. Cavalry Association* 60 (April 1906): 663-668.

"Military Notes." The Journal of the Royal United Service Institution 333 (November 1905): 1327-1334.

_____. *The Journal of the Royal United Service Institution* 335 (June 1906): 126-136.

_____. *The Journal of the Royal United Service Institution* 336 (February 1906): 248-249.

Moses, Andrew. "Use of the 12-inch Mortar in the Land Defense of Coast Fortifications." *Journal of the United States Artillery* 3 (May-June 1907): 232-237.

Neznamov, Colonel. "Teachings of the Russo-Japanese War." *Journal des Sciences Militaires* (March 1906). Translated by William Lassiter in *Journal of the United States Artillery* 3 (May-June 1906): 298-313.

Nidoine, Serge. "The Russian Calvary During the Russo-Japanese War." *Journal des Sciences Militaries* (August 1905). Translated by Herschel Tupes in *Journal of U.S. Cavalry Association* 64 (April 1907): 684-742.

Niessel, Major. "Cooperation of Infantry and Artillery in Combat." Translated by William Snow in *Journal of the United States Infantry* 5. (March 1909): 711-755.

Novikov, Colonel. "Questions of Artillery Tactics from the Experiences of the Russo-Japanese War." Translated by Fox Conner in *Journal of the United States Infantry Association* 4 (January 1908): 608-636.

Orr, G., Captain. "A Precis of "A Study of the Russo-Japanese War." by Chasseur," *TheJournal of the United Services Institution of India* 162 (January 1906): 18-26.

_____. "A Precis of "A Study of the Russo-Japanese War (Part 2)" by Chasseur," *The Journal of the United Services Institution of India* 163 (April 1906): 151-160.

_____. "Some Moral Factors in War." *The Journal of the United Services Institution of India* 180 (July 1910): 407-413.

Parker, John,Captain. "Progress in Machine Gun Development." *Journal of the United States Infantry Association* 1 (July 1908): 3-13.

Pottinger, E. "The Russo-Japanese War." *The Journal of the United Service Institute of India* 158 (January 1905): 72-84.

"Precis of Foreign Military Papers." *The Journal of the United Service Institution of India* 165 (October 1906): 455-456.

"Precis of Foreign Military Papers, German Papers." *The Journal of the United Service Institution of India* 169 (October 1907): 515-518.

"Precis of Foreign Military Papers, Italian Papers." *The Journal of the United Service Institution of India* 169 (October 1907): 523-537.

"Precis of Foreign Military Papers, Italian Papers." *The Journal of the United Service Institution of India* 174 (January 1909): 132-139.

"Precis of Foreign Military Papers." *The Journal of the United Service Institution of India* 175 (April 1909): 249-250.

"Precis of Foreign Military Papers, Italian Papers." *The Journal of the United Service Institution of India* 175 (April 1909): 264-271.

"Precis of Foreign Military Papers, Russian Papers." *The Journal of the United Service Institution of India* 178 (January 1910): 179-180.

"The Present Status of the Equipment of the Armies of the World with Machine-guns." *Beheft 79 zur Internationalen Revue uber die gesamten Armeen und Flotten* (October 1906), Translated by Oliver Spaulding in *Journal of the United States Infantry Association* 1 (July 1906): 144-163.

"Professional Notes, Damaged Russian Warships at Port Arthur." *Journal of the United States Artillery* 2 (September-October 1905): 174-178.

"Professional Notes, Lessons of the Russo-Japanese War: Armament." *Journal of the United States Artillery* 2 (September-October 1905): 172-174.

"Professional Notes, Notes on the Defense of Port Arthur." *Journal of the United States Artillery* 2 (May-June 1905): 307-308.

"Professional Notes, Notes on Field Artillery Material, 1905." *Journal of the United States Artillery* 2 (September-October 1905): 167-169.

"Professional Notes, Operations of the Artillery and Engineers at the Siege of PortArthur." *Journal of the United States Artillery* 2 (March-April 1905): 205-209.

Reichmann, Carl. "Chances in War." *Journal of the United States Infantry Association,* 1 (July 1906): 4-29.

Reilly, Henry. "Machine Gun Organization." *Journal of U.S. Cavalry Association* 72 (April 1909): 798-814.

_____. "Port Arthur." *Journal of U.S. Cavalry Association* 63 (January 1907):399-442.

Senior, H., Major. "Precis of Foreign Military Papers." *The Journal of the United Service Institute of India* 163 (April 1906): 194-198.

"The Service of Communications in the Light of the Experience of the Russo-Japanese War." Translated from *Russki Invalid* in *The Journal of the Royal United Service Institution* 365 (July 1908): 968-970.

Slocum, S. "Target Practice, Russia." *Journal of the United States Infantry Association,* 4 (April 1905): 105-110.

Taylor, N., Lieutenant. "The Battle of Mukden." *The Journal of the Royal United Service Institution* 176 (July 1909): 349-359.

Thuillier, H. "The Siege of Port Arthur." *The Journal of the United ServiceInstitute of India* 174 (January 1909): 53-74.

Vincent, B., Captain. "Artillery in the Manchurian Campaign." *The Journal of the Royal United Service Institution* 359 (January 1908): 28-53.

Vuilleumier, E. "Infantry Versus Machine Guns." Translated by I. Phillipson in *Journal of the United States Infantry Association* 3 (January 1907): 143-169.

"What Lessons Can the Cavalry Draw from the Russo-Japanese War?" *Militar-Wochenblatt* (December 1906), Translated by Walter Kruger in *Journal of U.S. Cavalry Association* 65 (July 1907): 122-135.

Wisser, John. "German Ideas on Tactics." *Journal of the United States Infantry* 3 (November 1910): 377-388.

Wood, E. "Gold Medal Prize Essay, 1907." *The Journal of the United Service Institution of India* 169 (October 1907): 401-433.

Wood, Oliver. "Target Practice – Japan." *Journal of the United States InfantryAssociation* 4 (April 1905): 111-121.

Wrangel, Gustav. "The Cavalry in the East Asiatic Campaign." Translated by Harry Bellin *Journal of U.S. Cavalry Association* 68 (January 1908): 451-500.

Yoda, Lieutenant Colonel. "Modern Tendencies in Strategy and Tactics as Shown in the Campaigns in the Far East." *Kaikosha Kiji* 352 (December 1906) Translated by E. Calthrop in *The Journal of the Royal United Service Institution* 353 (July 1907): 854-871.

Unpublished Materials

Andrus, Clift. An Outline of GEN Fujii's Estimate of the Russian Army at the Beginning of the Russo Japanese War, Group Report, 1935, Special Collections, Combined Arms Research Library, Fort Leavenworth, Kansas.

Baldwin, Kurt. The psychology, training, strength and armament of the Russian Soldier and Army, Group Report, 1931, Special Collections, Combined Arms Research Library, Fort Leavenworth, Kansas.

Bratton, Rufas, The Organization and Activities of the Intelligence Service of theJapanese Second Army, Group Report, 1931, Special Collections, Combined Arms Research Library, Fort Leavenworth, Kansas.

Burnell, Ray. The Russian Estimate of the Japanese Army, Group Report, 1931, Special Collections, Combined Arms Research Library, Fort Leavenworth, Kansas.

Ellis, Arthur. Compare the Russian and Japanese Services of Military Intelligence (G-2) to include May 2, 1904, Group Report, 1930, Special Collections, Combined Arms Research Library, Fort Leavenworth, Kansas.

Duncan, Early. Plans and Operations of the Japanese Fourth Army, 1 July--27 August 1904, Group Report, 1931, Special Collections, Combined Arms Research Library, Fort Leavenworth, Kansas.

Green, James. Comparison of the Uses of Infantry by the Russians and Japanese during the Battle of Wa-Fan-Gou, Group Report 1931, Special Collections, Combined Arms Research Library, Fort Leavenworth, Kansas.

Hossfeld, H., Translator, The Russo-Japanese War, from supplements to the *Marine Rundschau* (1904-1906), 1906, Special Collections, Combined Arms Research Library, Fort Leavenworth, Kansas.

Howland, C. The Russo-Japanese War, Eight Lectures by Colonel C. R. Howland, 1920-1921, Special Collections, Combined Arms Research Library, Fort Leavenworth, Kansas.

Janin, Pierre. Notes on the Tactics of the Russian and Japanese Armies during the Campaign of Manchuria. *Revue d Infantrerie*. Translated by Arthur Williams, n.d., Special Collections, Combined Arms Research Library, Fort Leavenworth, Kansas.

Kuhn, Joseph, Report on the Operations of the Japanese Armies during the Russo-Japanese War. n.d., Special Collections, Combined Arms Research Library, Fort Leavenworth, Kansas.

Maguire, H. Why Did Russia Lose Her War with Japan? Individual Report, 1930, Special Collections, Combined Arms Research Library, Fort Leavenworth, Kansas.

Niessel, Captain. Tactical Lessons Derived from the Russo-Japanese War. Translated by G. Bartlett, n.d., Special Collections, Combined Arms Research Library, Fort Leavenworth, Kansas.

Lectures on the Russo-Japanese War, Officers of the Japanese General Staff, Translated by the American Embassy, Tokyo. Special Collections, Combined Arms Research Library, Fort Leavenworth, Kansas, 1906.

Riggs, K. Lectures: Russo-Japanese War, First Lecture, n.d., Special Collections, Combined Arms Research Library, Fort Leavenworth, Kansas.

_____. Lectures: Russo-Japanese War, Second Lecture, n.d., Special Collections, Combined Arms Research Library, Fort Leavenworth, Kansas.

_____. Lectures: Russo-Japanese War, Third Lecture, n.d., Special Collections, Combined Arms Research Library, Fort Leavenworth, Kansas.

_____. Lectures: Russo-Japanese War, Fourth Lecture, n.d., Special Collections, Combined Arms Research Library, Fort Leavenworth, Kansas.

_____. Lectures: Russo-Japanese War, Seventh Lecture, n.d., Special Collections, Combined Arms Research Library, Fort Leavenworth, Kansas.

_____. Lectures: Russo-Japanese War, Eighth Lecture, n.d., Special Collections, Combined Arms Research Library, Fort Leavenworth, Kansas.

Saul, Leslie. Why did Russia Lose her War with Japan?, Individual Report, 1930, Special Collections, Combined Arms Research Library, Fort Leavenworth, Kansas.

Swift, Ira. Historical Analysis of Envelopment in the Battles of; The Franco-Prussian War, The Russo-Japanese War, The World War, Individual Report, 1935, Special Collections, Combined Arms Research Library, Fort Leavenworth, Kansas.

Ware, J. Discussion of the Influence of the Trans-Siberian Railroad on the Plans and Operations of the Russo-Japanese War of 1904-1905, Individual Report, 1931, Special Collections, Combined Arms Research Library, Fort Leavenworth, Kansas.

Washington, William. Japanese Estimates of the Russian Army, Group Report, 1931, Special Collections, Combined Arms Research Library, Fort Leavenworth, Kansas.

Weber, R. The Russo-Japanese War. *Revue Militaire Suisse*. Translated by S. Bell, 1906, Special Collections, Combined Arms Research Library, Fort Leavenworth, Kansas.

CPSIA information can be obtained
at www.ICGtesting.com
Printed in the USA
LVOW03s1025080416
482750LV00013B/171/P